ISABEL'S CANTINA

BOLD LATIN FLAVORS FROM THE NEW CALIFORNIA KITCHEN

ISABEL CRUZ

CLARKSON POTTER/PUBLISHERS
NEW YORK

Published in the United States by Clarkson Potter/Publishers, an
imprint of the Crown Publishing Group, a division of Random House,
Inc., New York.
www.crownpublishing.com
www.clarksonpotter.com

Clarkson N. Potter is a trademark and Potter and colophon are registered
trademarks of Random House, Inc.

Library of Congress Cataloging-in-Publication Data
Cruz, Isabel.
    Isabel's Cantina: bold Latin flavors from the new California kitchen /
Isabel Cruz.—1st ed.
        p. cm.
    Includes index.
    1. Cookery, Latin American.   2. Cookery—California.   I. Title.
TX716.A1C78   2007
641.59794—dc22   2006028776

ISBN 978-0-307-35274-3

Printed in China

Design by Laura Palese

10   9   8   7   6   5   4   3   2   1

First Edition

TO THE
**THREE MEN
IN MY LIFE:
ROBERT,
RYAN,**
and **WILLIAM**

CONTENTS

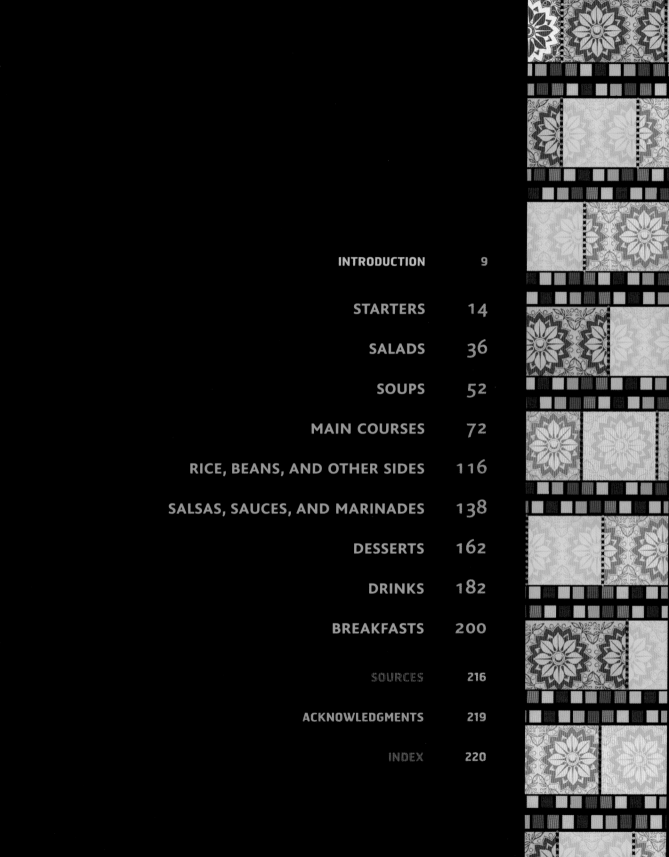

INTRODUCTION

I GREW UP IN A
PUERTO RICAN FAMILY
IN A LOS ANGELES NEIGHBORHOOD
FILLED WITH IMMIGRANTS.

Our neighbors were from Cuba, Mexico, Peru, Japan, and Thailand. One day when I was eight, I brought a new friend home from school. I was embarrassed by my father's thick accent and even more embarrassed when he served up a fish stew smothered in cilantro for dinner. Not many people knew what cilantro was back then. To my surprise, my friend, who was half Japanese, loved it. She, too, had grown up eating food that was "different." We're still friends to this day.

My parents used to throw these wonderful, crazy, loud parties that started early in the day with my aunts and grandmothers cooking up a storm. There would be pots of black beans, onions, garlic, and cilantro simmering on the stove; roasted chicken with lemon; mounds of white rice; plantains every way you could imagine them; dark rum; and even darker espresso. My father started inviting all of the neighbors (so they wouldn't complain about the noise) and pretty soon everyone began

bringing amazing dishes to our house, everything from posole to pad thai. When the dancing finally wound down in the wee hours of the night, we'd fry up some eggs and serve them over leftover arroz con gandules.

At our parties, I always stuck around the kitchen watching the women cook—to me, the kitchen was where the real action was. I saw the women's passion for sharing delicious food with their families and friends. It gave them a great sense of pride, but it also gave them a way to pass down family and cultural traditions. And I learned a thing or two about all of these different cuisines.

Many years later, when I found myself a single mother with two kids to feed and no formal education to fall back on, I relied on what I knew best, the things that I had learned in my childhood kitchen. Naively, I opened a restaurant in San Diego, California. Improbably, it thrived. I shared my take on the simple Latin comfort foods I grew up with—the easy-to-prepare meals I cooked every night for my boys—mixed with a little bit of the Asian influences I developed a taste for in my old LA neighborhood.

I began preparing the roasted chicken that the women in my family often made, this time for the friendly faces who visited my first restaurant. It was a block from the beach, and knowing how body-conscious my customers were (and wanting to stay fit myself!), I decided to lighten things up—making my black beans and rice with a short-grain brown rice instead of white or preparing *albóndigas* soup with turkey meatballs instead of beef. I found that if I was creative, there was no reason for the flavor to suffer just because I cut calories or fat. In fact, sometimes a seemingly incongruous dash of soy sauce was just what a dish needed to pull everything together.

And it's easy to be creative with fantastically fresh California produce and inspiration from the Latin and Asian cuisines I grew up with as a kid.

MANGOES, LIMES, COCONUT, CHILE PEPPERS, MINT, GARLIC, GINGER, AND CILANTRO

—these are just some of the flavorful ingredients these cuisines share, making mixing and matching new irresistible combinations fun and successful. These are my flavor building-blocks, my go-to ingredients for making fresh sauces and salsas like Cilantro-Garlic Mojo or Avocado Salsa Cruda, which add layers of sophisticated and satisfying flavor. (That way, I can indulge when I want to without piling on the pounds— Flourless Chocolate-Ginger Cake and Coconut Flan are my personal weaknesses!) These sauces and salsas can transform almost any dish. Salmon Cakes with Chipotle-Corn Salsa can just as easily be served with Easy Española Tomato Sauce or Papaya-Mango-Mint Salsa, depending on your mood and what you have on hand.

I now own five restaurants with my husband along the West Coast: Isabel's Cantina, the Coffee Cup, Dragonfly, Seaside Cantina, and Isabel.

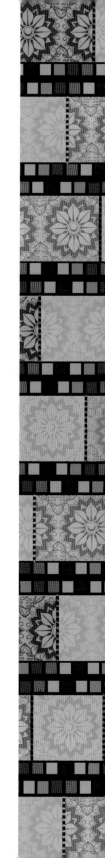

FOR ME, A CANTINA IS A WARM, NEIGHBORHOOD PLACE WHERE PEOPLE GATHER AT ANY HOUR TO TALK ABOUT THEIR DAY.

To that end, we serve breakfast, lunch, and dinner in nearly all of my restaurants. From the breathtaking shores of La Jolla, California, to the earthy beauty of Portland, Oregon, every day I share with my customers my take on Latin food that both tastes great and is good for you. I am always thrilled to win over hungry diners with my style of cooking, so I am excited to share these recipes with you in my first book.

In these pages, you'll find the shortcuts that took me years to figure out, and learn that fast weeknight meals don't have to mean fast food, that big celebration-type meals don't have to take all day to make, that Latin food can be healthy and light and still be delicious, and that today's Latin food is a blend of the cultures that surround it.

I hope you'll enjoy these recipes and cooking delicious, healthful meals for the important people in your life as much as I do.

SALUD!

STARTERS

MY IDEAL STARTER IS A COLORFUL BITE OR LITTLE DISH THAT GOES PERFECTLY WITH FUN COCKTAILS (SEE DRINKS, PAGE 182) OR WINE.

Think Steak Skewers with Mint Mojo or Salmon Cakes with Chipotle-Corn Salsa. Sometimes these kick off a party, and other times they are the party. Originally from Spain, tapas (little snacks served with drinks) have become a way of life all over Latin America, and here in the States we can't seem to get enough of them. I love the trend of making a bunch of little things for dinner with friends to shake up the usual appetizer, main course, dessert routine.

Whether you serve these recipes as little treats before the main event or give them center stage, remember to keep the whole menu in mind. If you have a light meal planned, you can go for something a little richer to start (may I suggest Tostones with Baked Carnitas and Avocado?). Since starters are just a few bites, they're a good place to indulge without it being the end of the world. Enjoy!

SALT COD AND OLIVE
SALSA FRESCA 17

**SEARED TUNA WONTONS
WITH AVOCADO
SALSA CRUDA 18**

SHRIMP BITES WRAPPED
IN GREENS 20

TOSTONES WITH
BAKED CARNITAS AND
AVOCADO 21

**SALMON CAKES WITH
CHIPOTLE-CORN SALSA 24**

SIMPLE CEVICHE 27

**SOPES WITH
BLACK BEANS 28**

**SEARED SCALLOPS WITH
ROASTED TOMATO, SAFFRON,
AND CAPER SAUCE 32**

EASY TURKEY
EMPANADAS 33

**CHICKEN AND LETTUCE
WRAPS WITH
CILANTRO-LIME SAUCE 34**

STEAK SKEWERS WITH
MINT MOJO 35

SALT COD
AND OLIVE
SALSA FRESCA

SERVES 4

4 OUNCES SALT COD

3 TABLESPOONS OLIVE OIL

½ MEDIUM RED ONION, FINELY DICED

2 PLUM TOMATOES, DICED

¼ CUP SLICED GREEN OLIVES

¼ CUP SLICED KALAMATA OLIVES

½ AVOCADO, DICED

TORTILLA CHIPS, CRACKERS, OR SMALL TOASTS, FOR SERVING

LIME WEDGES, FOR SERVING

ISABEL'S tip

Originally, salting and drying were a way of preserving fish on the long voyage from the North Atlantic to the Mediterranean. Now, even with modern refrigeration, salt cod is sought after for its great flavor. In its dried form, it keeps in cool, dry storage for a long time and doesn't need to be frozen. Salt cod can be found in most ethnic and specialty food stores.

A change from the usual chips and salsa, this feisty combination features salt cod, tomatoes, red onion, olives, and avocado and is perfect for topping chips, crackers, or toast. A Cucumber Margarita (page 192) would be the ideal companion.

While this is a simple dish to make, the salt cod needs to soak in the refrigerator for two days, so advance planning is required.

Rinse the salt cod under running water. Submerge the fish in a bowl of cold water and soak for 2 days in the refrigerator, changing the water once. Remove the salt cod and rinse well under running water.

Preheat the oven to 350°F.

Blot the fish dry with paper towels. Rub the whole fish, top and bottom, with 1 tablespoon of the olive oil, place in a baking dish, and bake until the fish flakes easily when prodded with a fork, about 5 minutes. Remove from the oven and set aside to cool.

Use your fingers to flake the fish, discarding any bones or skin. Combine the shredded salt cod with the onion, tomatoes, olives, avocado, and the remaining 2 tablespoons olive oil in a small bowl and toss gently. Chill for at least 1 hour or overnight.

Serve with tortilla chips for dipping and lime wedges for squeezing on top.

SEARED TUNA WONTONS
WITH AVOCADO SALSA CRUDA

SERVES 10
as an hors d'oeuvre

3 TABLESPOONS CANOLA OR PEANUT OIL

1 POUND SUSHI-GRADE TUNA STEAK, PREFERABLY YELLOWFIN (ABOUT 1 INCH THICK)

10 WONTON SQUARES, EACH CUT INTO 2 RECTANGLES

¼ CUP SWEET SOY SAUCE (PAGE 159)

WASABI CREAM (RECIPE FOLLOWS), OPTIONAL

AVOCADO SALSA CRUDA (PAGE 143)

These open-faced small bites give a little nod to Japan but are 100 percent California. They're one of the most popular appetizers at my restaurants because they're just delicious. I whip them up at home for guests because they couldn't be easier to make.

Yellowfin tuna, also known as ahi, is my preference here, but buy the freshest tuna you can find. Look for a deep red color, firm healthy texture, and good clean smell. Wonton squares are sold in packages, refrigerated, in Asian groceries and gourmet markets. In a pinch, you can substitute a thin rice cracker.

In a large nonstick sauté pan, heat the oil over medium-high heat until hot but not smoking. Sear the tuna steak for 20 seconds on each side until well browned. Transfer to a cutting board, let cool, then wrap in plastic wrap and refrigerate for 1 hour to make it easier to cut.

Preheat the oven to 325°F.

Spread out the wonton wrappers on a baking sheet. Bake until crisp and lightly browned, about 8 minutes. Remove from the oven and set aside to cool.

Place the wonton rectangles on a serving platter. Using a sharp, straight-bladed knife, cut the tuna against the grain into ¼-inch-thick slices. Top each rectangle with a slice of tuna and drizzle the Sweet Soy Sauce and wasabi cream over the top. Add a dollop of avocado salsa and serve immediately.

WASABI CREAM

MAKES 1/3 CUP

1 TABLESPOON WASABI POWDER

1/4 CUP SOUR CREAM
OR PLAIN YOGURT

In a small bowl, whisk the wasabi powder with 1 1/2 tablespoons cold water until smooth. Add the sour cream and continue whisking to form a creamy green sauce. Store, covered, in the refrigerator for up to 1 week.

SHRIMP BITES
WRAPPED IN GREENS

SERVES 6
as an hors d'oeuvre

SERVES 6
as an hors d'oeuvre

6 MEDIUM SHRIMP, PEELED AND DEVEINED

1 TABLESPOON OLIVE OIL

KOSHER SALT

FRESHLY GROUND BLACK PEPPER

ABOUT 3 COLLARD GREEN LEAVES, CUT INTO TWELVE 2-INCH SQUARES

1/2 CUP SHREDDED SWEETENED DRIED COCONUT, TOASTED (SEE BELOW)

1/2 CUP CHOPPED UNSALTED PEANUTS

2 INCHES FRESH GINGER, PEELED AND CUT INTO THIN MATCHSTICKS

2 THAI CHILES, THINLY SLICED INTO CIRCLES

GUAVA SAUCE (PAGE 155)

This is my take on *mieng kam*, a traditional Thai appetizer of shrimp wrapped with coconut, peanuts, and chiles in a leaf. I like to use raw collard greens as the wrappers for these spicy little snacks, which I drizzle with a little Guava Sauce to complete the hot-sweet Thai flavors while also bringing these bites further into the Latin realm. Prepare the ingredients in advance, and then assemble these at the last minute.

Heat a grill or medium sauté pan over medium-high heat. In a small bowl, toss the shrimp with the olive oil and season with salt and pepper. Add the shrimp to the pan and cook until firm and opaque, about 2 minutes per side. Remove from the heat and slice in half lengthwise. Set aside to cool.

Lay the collard green squares flat on a tray. Divide the shrimp halves among the greens and top each shrimp half with a sprinkle of toasted coconut, some peanuts and ginger matchsticks, and a few rings of chile. Serve the Guava Sauce in a bowl alongside the shrimp bites for drizzling on top.

■■■ **TO TOAST COCONUT:** *Preheat the oven to 350°F. Spread the coconut evenly on a baking sheet. Toast in the oven until the coconut turns golden brown, about 20 minutes, stirring after 10 minutes to toast evenly. Remove from the oven and set aside to cool completely. Store in an airtight container. For best flavor, use within 1 week.*

TOSTONES
WITH BAKED CARNITAS AND AVOCADO

SERVES 8
as an hors d'oeuvre
or 4 as an appetizer

1 POUND BONELESS PORK
SHOULDER, FAT TRIMMED

1½ TEASPOONS GROUND
CUMIN

1½ TEASPOONS DRIED
OREGANO

¾ TEASPOON KOSHER SALT,
PLUS EXTRA FOR SPRINKLING

¾ TEASPOON FRESHLY
GROUND BLACK PEPPER

2 GREEN PLANTAINS,
PEELED (SEE PAGE 22)

ABOUT 3 CUPS CANOLA OR
PEANUT OIL, FOR FRYING

1 AVOCADO, SLICED

½ CUP BASIC SALSA
(PAGE 141)

Plantains are one of my favorite ingredients because they are so versatile—they're great mashed, roasted, fried, and simmered in stews. One of the most traditional ways to prepare green plantains is to make tostones. The plantains are cooked twice, first to soften the flesh and then, after a quick smash with a *tostonera* or a mallet, they go back into the hot oil to fry to a golden crispness. While tostones are often served as a side dish, I also like to use them as a base for an hors d'oeuvre. These are wonderful as a passed snack at parties or as a special first course.

Because the tostones are rich, I pair them with baked spiced pork (carnitas), a fresh tomato salsa, and a little avocado to round things out. These are even better topped with a drizzle of fresh Cilantro Sauce (page 161). The carnitas can be cooked a day in advance, stored in the refrigerator, covered, and seared in a pan to reheat before serving.

Combine the cumin, oregano, salt, and pepper in a small bowl. Rub the seasoning on the pork, put the pork in a baking dish, and cover with plastic wrap. Refrigerate for at least 2 hours or overnight.

Preheat the oven to 350°F.

Remove the plastic wrap and cover the baking dish tightly with aluminum foil. Bake the pork for 45 to 55 minutes, until the meat is tender when pierced with a knife. Uncover and set aside to cool at least slightly.

Recipe continues

Increase the oven temperature to 425°F.

While the pork is cooking, cut each peeled plantain half into 4 pieces on the diagonal. Blot dry with paper towels.

In a large sauté pan, heat 2 inches of oil over medium heat until small bubbles begin to form on the bottom of the pan. (If you have a frying thermometer and want to use it, the temperature you are looking for is 325°F.) Working in batches, transfer the plantain pieces to the hot oil, placing one of the cut sides down, and cook until lightly golden and almost tender, about 3 minutes per side.

Remove the plantain slices from the oil to a paper-towel-lined plate. Place the plantain slices between 2 clean paper bags or pieces of parchment paper and smash with a mallet, rolling pin, or the bottom of a small sauté pan. The plantains should be pounded to about $1/4$ inch thick. If a plantain slice crumbles and won't flatten to $1/4$ inch, the batch needs further cooking before smashing.

Cut the pork into $1/2$-inch-thick slices. Drain any fat from the baking dish, return the pork to the dish, and return to the oven until lightly browned, 10 to 15 minutes.

Meanwhile, after smashing the plantains, raise the heat under the pan to medium-high (the oil should be around 350°F) and transfer the flattened slices back to the pan in batches. Cook them this time until golden brown, about 2 minutes per side. Transfer to paper towels to drain and then sprinkle with salt.

Arrange the tostones on a serving platter. Top each with a slice of avocado, slices of pork carnitas, and some salsa. Serve warm.

■■■ **TO PEEL GREEN PLANTAINS:** *Cut off the ends and then cut the plantain in half crosswise. Use a paring knife to score the skin in long slits down the sides. Soak in warm water for 20 minutes and then use a paring knife to peel the skin off in strips from top to bottom. Submerge the peeled plantain halves in salted water until ready to cook, then drain and cut as indicated in your recipe.*

SALMON CAKES
WITH CHIPOTLE-CORN SALSA

SERVES 6
as an appetizer

3 TABLESPOONS OLIVE OIL

1 1/2 POUNDS SALMON FILLETS

KOSHER SALT

FRESHLY GROUND BLACK
PEPPER

1 MEDIUM YELLOW ONION,
CHOPPED

4 GARLIC CLOVES, MINCED

1/4 CUP DRY WHITE WINE

3 LARGE EGGS

2 TABLESPOONS MAYONNAISE

2 1/2 CUPS PANKO

4 TABLESPOONS CANOLA OIL

CHIPOTLE-CORN SALSA
(PAGE 144)

These cakes are a little lighter than most, with no bread crumbs to bind them and only a light coating of panko (see page 93) on the outside to crisp them. A zesty corn salsa is a perfect accompaniment to the salmon cakes, but Papaya-Mango-Mint Salsa (page 76) would make a great variation. With either salsa, try drizzling Cilantro-Lime Sauce (page 161) on top to add some color and flavor.

If you're planning a party, these are a must. The salmon cakes can be prepared up to the point of cooking and then frozen in an airtight container. Thaw them in the refrigerator before cooking.

Preheat the oven to 350°F.

Drizzle a rimmed baking sheet with 2 tablespoons of the olive oil and smooth with your fingers to lightly coat the sheet. Season the salmon with salt and pepper and place, skin side down, on the prepared sheet. Bake until the flesh begins to flake when poked with a fork, 20 to 25 minutes. Remove from the oven and set aside to cool.

While the salmon is baking, heat the remaining 1 tablespoon olive oil in a small sauté pan over medium heat. Add the onion and garlic and cook until soft and translucent, about 3 minutes. Add the white wine and bring to a simmer. Cook for 4 minutes. Turn off the heat and set aside to cool.

Transfer the onion and garlic to a bowl and flake the salmon into the bowl, taking care to remove any remaining bones and leaving the skin behind on the baking sheet. Lightly beat 1 of

Recipe continues

the eggs and add to the bowl along with the mayonnaise. Season with salt and pepper. Combine by gently folding with a rubber spatula.

Line a baking tray with parchment paper. Using your hands, form the salmon mixture into 1$^1/_2$- to 2-inch round cakes that are 1$^1/_2$ to 2 inches thick. You should have about 12 cakes. Place the cakes on the baking sheet and then refrigerate for 10 minutes to help them firm up.

Lightly beat the remaining 2 eggs in a shallow bowl. Put the panko in a separate bowl. Dip the salmon cakes in the eggs and then dredge in the panko.

Heat 2 tablespoons of the canola oil in a large sauté pan over medium-high heat. When the oil is very hot but not smoking, transfer the coated salmon cakes to the pan and brown for 2 minutes. Flip the cakes, add the remaining 2 tablespoons oil to the pan, and brown for 2 minutes. Transfer the cakes to a baking sheet and bake in the oven to heat throughout, 10 to 15 minutes.

Serve warm with a dollop of Chipotle-Corn Salsa.

SIMPLE
CEVICHE

SERVES 4 TO 6

1 POUND SUSHI-GRADE TUNA STEAK, PREFERABLY YELLOWFIN, CUT INTO 1/4-INCH DICE

3/4 CUP LEMON JUICE (ABOUT 6 LEMONS)

1/2 CUP LIME JUICE (ABOUT 4 LIMES)

1 TO 2 RED SERRANO CHILES, TO TASTE, THINLY SLICED INTO CIRCLES

1/2 MEDIUM RED ONION, THINLY SLICED

2 GARLIC CLOVES, MINCED

1 TEASPOON KOSHER SALT

1 TEASPOON WASABI POWDER

1 MANGO, PEELED AND CUT INTO 1/2-INCH DICE

1/2 CUP CHOPPED FRESH MINT

The mango adds a little sweetness to this simple ceviche of meaty tuna, puckery citrus juices, fragrant mint, and fiery wasabi and chiles.

As the tuna is cooked only by the acid in the lemon and lime juices, make sure it is impeccably fresh.

In a medium bowl, gently toss the tuna with the lemon juice, lime juice, chiles, onion, garlic, and salt. Cover and refrigerate for 30 minutes.

Sprinkle the wasabi powder over the top and then mix together. Gently stir in the mango and mint. Serve immediately.

SOPES
WITH
BLACK
BEANS

SERVES 8
*as an appetizer
or 4 as a main course*

**ABOUT 2 CUPS
MASA HARINA**

**GRATED ZEST AND JUICE OF
2 LIMES**

**2 CUPS QUICK BLACK BEANS
(PAGE 121), WARMED**

**1 CUP ROASTED TOMATILLO
SAUCE (PAGE 148)**

2 CUPS SHREDDED LETTUCE

2 PLUM TOMATOES, DICED

**$\frac{1}{2}$ CUP SHREDDED
MONTEREY JACK CHEESE**

1 AVOCADO, SLICED

$\frac{1}{2}$ CUP SOUR CREAM

$\frac{1}{4}$ CUP FRESH CILANTRO

Sopes, or boats, are small tortillas filled much

like a tostada or taco. If you've ever wanted to learn how to make tortillas at home, this is a good place to start. Made with masa harina, a Mexican cornmeal flour made with lime available in Latin markets, these are smaller and thicker than traditional tortillas and cooked in a hot, dry skillet rather than fried. The fillings for sopes are endless, from grilled chicken to shrimp; think of them as a blank canvas and then get creative.

These make great party food because you just set everything out and guests get to customize their own sopes.

Place the masa harina, $1\frac{1}{2}$ cups water, and the lime zest and juice in the bowl of a standing mixer fitted with the paddle attachment. Mix on slow speed until a soft, Play-Doh–like dough forms. (Alternatively, combine the ingredients in a large bowl and knead with your hands.) Add a tablespoon or two of water or a little more masa if needed to give the right consistency. You can make the dough in advance to save time: Wrap the dough in plastic wrap and refrigerate for up to 2 days. Bring back to room temperature before using.

To make the sopes, pinch off golf-ball-size pieces of dough and roll into balls with your hands. You should have about 16 balls. Flatten them by placing each dough ball between two pieces of parchment or waxed paper and then pressing with a small plate. Ideally, they should be about 3 inches in diameter and about $\frac{1}{4}$ inch thick.

Recipe continues

Heat a flat griddle or large sauté pan over medium heat. As a trial, place 1 sope on the hot surface. (Like pancakes, the first ones are not usually the most perfect.) Cook until the sope begins to puff or to turn golden brown, 2 to 3 minutes, and then turn and cook the other side, 2 to 3 minutes.

The sopes should be warm and soft all the way through, but not raw. Adjust the heat as necessary and cook the remaining sopes (about 4 per batch). Keep finished sopes wrapped in a clean towel so they stay warm while you cook the rest.

Serve the warm sopes with the beans, tomatillo sauce, lettuce, tomatoes, cheese, avocado, sour cream, and cilantro in small bowls so your guests can fill theirs as they like.

EASY TURKEY EMPANADAS

SERVES 6
as an appetizer
or 2 as a main course

1 LARGE RED POTATO, PEELED
AND CUT INTO
¼-INCH SLICES

KOSHER SALT

2 TABLESPOONS OLIVE OIL

½ MEDIUM YELLOW
ONION, DICED

3 GARLIC CLOVES, MINCED

1½ TEASPOONS
GROUND CUMIN

8 OUNCES GROUND TURKEY

¼ CUP DRAINED SLICED
GREEN OLIVES WITH
PIMIENTOS

¼ CUP DRAINED CAPERS

FRESHLY GROUND
BLACK PEPPER

SIX 6-INCH FLOUR TORTILLAS

2 LARGE EGGS,
LIGHTLY BEATEN

EASY ESPAÑOLA TOMATO
SAUCE (PAGE 145)

When I was a kid, my dad loved to make empanadas, but the dough would stress him out (and made the kitchen look like a tornado had hit it). Then he figured out that store-bought flour tortillas could form the pockets for the empanada filling. He turned into an empanada-making fiend, coming up with all sorts of fillings for these little pies.

These are the empanadas that I make with my kids, using ground turkey. They're light, delicious, and perfect for almost any meal. And the kitchen stays pretty clean, too!

Put the potato in a small saucepan and cover with salted water. Bring to a boil over medium-high heat and cook until tender, about 5 minutes. Drain well and set aside.

While the potato is cooking, heat the olive oil in a large sauté pan over medium-high heat. Add the onion and garlic and cook until soft and translucent, about 3 minutes. Add the cumin, stir to combine, and then add the ground turkey. Use a wooden spoon to break up the meat, and cook until the turkey is no longer pink, 5 to 7 minutes. Use a slotted spoon to transfer the mixture to a medium bowl. Add the potato, olives, and capers and season lightly with salt and pepper. Toss to combine.

Preheat the oven to 350°F. Place the tortillas on a clean work surface. Brush the edges with the egg wash. Divide the filling among the bottom halves of the tortillas, and then fold over the top halves to form half-moons. Crimp the edges with a fork. Brush the tops of the empanadas with the remaining egg wash. Arrange on a baking sheet and bake for 20 to 25 minutes, until the tops are golden brown.

Serve warm with small bowls of the tomato sauce alongside.

SEARED SCALLOPS
WITH ROASTED TOMATO, SAFFRON, AND CAPER SAUCE

SERVES 4
as an appetizer
or 2 as a main course

**5 PLUM TOMATOES, CUT INTO
¾-INCH CHUNKS**

6 TABLESPOONS OLIVE OIL

**¼ CUP THINLY SLICED
SHALLOTS**

4 GARLIC CLOVES, MINCED

1 CUP DRY WHITE WINE

PINCH OF SAFFRON

**2 TABLESPOONS DRAINED
CAPERS**

**½ TEASPOON FRESH
LEMON JUICE**

8 JUMBO SEA SCALLOPS

KOSHER SALT

**FRESHLY GROUND BLACK
PEPPER**

**2 VINE-RIPENED TOMATOES,
THINLY SLICED**

ISABEL's tip

Saffron is the world's most expensive spice. Lucky for us the tiny threads are powerful and only a pinch is needed to add aroma, flavor, and color. Saffron is available in most ethnic markets and the specialty foods section of larger supermarkets.

This simple-to-prepare dish yields amazing results. The sauce is the secret—it has a deep tomato flavor, enhanced by threads of saffron and salty capers, a great counterpart to the silky rich scallops.

Preheat the oven to 350°F.

Spread out the plum tomatoes on a rimmed baking sheet and drizzle lightly with 2 tablespoons of the olive oil. Roast in the oven until the tomatoes appear shrunken and brighter in color, about 30 minutes. Remove from the oven and set aside to cool.

Heat 2 tablespoons of the olive oil in a medium sauté pan over medium heat until hot but not smoking. Add the shallots and garlic and cook for 1 minute. Add the white wine and saffron. Bring to a simmer and cook for 4 minutes. Add the roasted tomatoes, the capers, and the lemon juice. Stir well and cook for 2 minutes more. Turn off the heat, cover, and keep warm while you cook the scallops.

Heat the remaining 2 tablespoons olive oil in a medium sauté pan over high heat. Pat the scallops dry with paper towels and season lightly on both sides with salt and pepper. Place the scallops in the pan and cook, undisturbed, for 2 minutes. Turn them over and brown the other side for 2 minutes. The scallops should be well browned and feel firm on the outside but give a little in the center.

Place the sliced fresh tomatoes on plates. Sprinkle lightly with salt and top with the seared scallops. Spoon the warm tomato-saffron mixture over each serving.

CHICKEN AND LETTUCE WRAPS
WITH CILANTRO-LIME SAUCE

SERVES 4
as an appetizer
or 2 as a main course

2 TABLESPOONS OLIVE OIL

TWO 8-OUNCE BONELESS, SKINLESS CHICKEN BREAST HALVES, CUT INTO 1/2-INCH DICE

1/2 TEASPOON KOSHER SALT

1/2 TEASPOON FRESHLY GROUND BLACK PEPPER

8 LETTUCE LEAVES, PREFERABLY GREEN LEAF LETTUCE

CILANTRO-LIME SAUCE (PAGE 161)

1/2 MEDIUM RED ONION, DICED

1 VINE-RIPENED TOMATO, DICED

1 AVOCADO, DICED

These are hot and cool, filling and refreshing, crunchy and tender, all at the same time. Serve these as starters, or with brown rice and some salsa as a summertime main dish.

Heat the oil in a large sauté pan over medium heat. Sprinkle the chicken with the salt and pepper. Put the chicken in the pan and cook, stirring, until the chicken is lightly browned and cooked through, 5 to 7 minutes.

To serve, top each lettuce leaf with some chicken, a drizzle of Cilantro-Lime Sauce, and a sprinkling of onion, tomato, and avocado. Fold the lettuce around the filling and serve immediately.

STEAK SKEWERS WITH MINT MOJO

SERVES 6
*as an appetizer
or 4 as a main course*

½ CUP TERIYAKI SAUCE

½ CUP CANOLA OR
PEANUT OIL

4 GARLIC CLOVES, MINCED

1 SKIRT STEAK
(1 TO 1½ POUNDS)

ABOUT TWELVE 12-INCH
BAMBOO SKEWERS, SOAKED
IN WATER FOR 30 MINUTES

MINT MOJO (PAGE 152)

On some evenings, I make this recipe at home and serve it as an appetizer. On other nights, I make a little rice and Aspirations with Red Bell Pepper and Chile Flakes (page 137) and I call it dinner. Either way, everyone is very happy.

Combine the teriyaki sauce, oil, and garlic in a glass baking dish (or large resealable plastic bag). Whisk together to combine.

With a sharp, straight-bladed knife, cut the meat across the grain into thin slices. Place the meat in the baking dish and turn to coat with the marinade. Cover with plastic wrap and refrigerate overnight.

Heat your grill to high. Alternatively, heat a grill pan over medium-high heat for 3 minutes. Thread the slices onto the skewers, piercing each slide of meat 3 or 4 times with the skewer and using about 2 slices per skewer. Grill until hot and cooked through, about 1 minute per side.

Transfer the skewers to a serving platter. Serve with the Mint Mojo in a small bowl alongside.

SALADS

THE LATIN SALADS I GREW UP WITH—

THE ONES YOU STILL FIND IN SMALL MOM-AND-POP RESTAURANTS AND MANY HOMES— WERE TYPICALLY QUITE SIMPLE:

lettuce, sliced tomatoes, maybe some thinly sliced red onion, and, if we were lucky, some ripe avocado slices.

They never hit the table in my childhood home without their accompanying caddy of olive oil and vinegar in clear bottles with shiny metal tops and shakers of salt and pepper.

As far as the lettuce and vegetables go, I've expanded my horizons in recipes such as Oven-Roasted Vegetable Salad with Sofrito Vinaigrette and Blood Orange and Mango Salad with Balsamic-Ginger Vinaigrette while still keeping everything simple and fresh. And I now prefer slightly more composed (but never complicated) dressings that can be varied, like Lemon Vinaigrette (page 156), with the addition of a spice (to make Cumin Vinaigrette) or by swapping the acid (to make Lime Vinaigrette), to shake things up a little. But one thing has stayed the same: I still use olive oil as the base for all of my salad dressings. Beyond its healing and antiaging virtues, it simply has the best flavor for greens and crisp vegetables.

ORANGE AND
FENNEL SALAD 39

OVEN-ROASTED VEGETABLE
SALAD WITH SOFRITO
VINAIGRETTE 40

BLOOD ORANGE
AND MANGO SALAD WITH
BALSAMIC-GINGER
VINAIGRETTE 42

JÍCAMA, CUCUMBER,
AND RADISH SALAD WITH
LIME VINAIGRETTE 45

CORN AND
AVOCADO SALAD 46

SPANISH POTATO SALAD 47

HEIRLOOM TOMATO AND
RED ONION SALAD WITH
CILANTRO SAUCE 48

BLUE CHEESE AND WALNUT
SALAD WITH CUMIN
VINAIGRETTE 50

WATERCRESS, RADICCHIO,
ENDIVE, AND
AVOCADO SALAD 51

ORANGE
AND FENNEL
SALAD

SERVES 4

2 NAVEL ORANGES

1 LARGE FENNEL BULB, OUTER LAYER REMOVED, THINLY SLICED

3 CUPS MIXED LETTUCES

ORANGE-OREGANO DRESSING (PAGE 154)

KOSHER SALT

FRESHLY GROUND BLACK PEPPER

ISABEL'S tip

If you have a mandoline, now is the perfect time to use it to get paper-thin fennel slices. The Japanese Benriner is inexpensive, easy to clean, and friendly looking, unlike the big, heavy professional models.

This is a refreshing and elegant salad that everyone will love, including the cook, because it is so easy to make. Orange-Oregano Dressing enhances these bright fresh flavors and adds a very Latin touch.

Slice off the top and bottom of each orange. Stand each orange on one end and, following the curve of the fruit, slice the peel away from top to bottom in wide strips. When all the peel and pith have been removed, slice each orange into $1/4$-inch-thick rounds and place the slices in a large bowl.

Add the fennel and lettuce to the bowl and toss gently to combine. Drizzle the dressing over, toss, and then transfer to serving plates. Sprinkle with salt and pepper.

OVEN-ROASTED VEGETABLE SALAD
WITH SOFRITO VINAIGRETTE

SERVES 6

6 PLUM TOMATOES, EACH CUT
INTO 4 WEDGES

1 LARGE ZUCCHINI, HALVED
LENGTHWISE AND SLICED

1 LARGE RED BELL PEPPER, CUT
INTO THIN STRIPS

KOSHER SALT

FRESHLY GROUND BLACK
PEPPER

5 TABLESPOONS OLIVE OIL

4 PORTOBELLO MUSHROOM
CAPS, EACH CUT
INTO 6 PIECES

1 TABLESPOON BALSAMIC
VINEGAR

6 CUPS MIXED LETTUCES

SOFRITO VINAIGRETTE
(PAGE 147)

Oven-roasted vegetables give heft to a salad of mixed greens. When paired with a vinaigrette made with roasted bell peppers, onion, and garlic, the combo takes on a deep Latin flavor. Char-grilled shrimp or chicken can be added to boost this to main-course material.

Preheat the oven to 350°F.

Place the tomato wedges, zucchini, and bell pepper on a rimmed baking sheet. Sprinkle with salt and pepper and then drizzle with 2 tablespoons of the olive oil. Toss with your hands. Roast in the oven for about 45 minutes, or until the vegetables are very tender. Set aside to cool.

While the vegetables are roasting, heat the remaining
3 tablespoons olive oil in a medium sauté pan over medium
heat until hot but not smoking. Add the mushrooms to the pan
and allow them to cook for about 2 minutes, turning once.
Drizzle with the balsamic vinegar and season with salt and
pepper. Cook the mushrooms for an additional 1 to 2 minutes
to caramelize. The mushrooms should be soft and well browned.
Set aside to cool.

To serve, divide the lettuces among 6 plates. Arrange the grilled
vegetables over the lettuces and drizzle the vinaigrette over the
top. Serve immediately.

ISABEL'S **tip**

Because the vegetables are
served at room temperature,
they can be made ahead of time.
If making them more than a few
hours in advance, cover and
refrigerate them. Bring to room
temperature before serving.

BLOOD ORANGE AND MANGO SALAD
WITH BALSAMIC-GINGER VINAIGRETTE

SERVES 4

2 BLOOD ORANGES

3 CUPS MESCLUN GREENS

1 LARGE MANGO, PEELED AND THINLY SLICED

KOSHER SALT

FRESHLY GROUND BLACK PEPPER

BALSAMIC-GINGER VINAIGRETTE (RECIPE FOLLOWS)

This blend of ingredients is Latin in spirit:

The colors are vibrant and the flavors bold. Serve this salad on its own or as a companion to deeply flavored meats. If blood oranges aren't in season, the regular type will do nicely.

Slice off the top and bottom of each orange. Stand each orange on one end and, following the curve of the fruit, slice the peel away from top to bottom in wide strips. When all the peel and pith have been removed, slice each orange into 1/2-inch-thick rounds.

Spread the greens over a serving platter. Arrange the mango and orange slices on the greens. Salt and pepper to taste and drizzle with the vinaigrette just before serving.

BALSAMIC-GINGER VINAIGRETTE

MAKES 1/2 CUP

1/4 CUP BALSAMIC VINEGAR

1 TABLESPOON MINCED FRESH GINGER

1 TABLESPOON PACKED LIGHT BROWN SUGAR

1/4 CUP EXTRA-VIRGIN OLIVE OIL

KOSHER SALT

FRESHLY GROUND BLACK PEPPER

Combine the vinegar, ginger, and brown sugar in a small bowl. Drizzle the olive oil into the bowl in a steady stream while whisking to form an emulsion. Season with salt and pepper to taste. The vinaigrette can be stored covered in the refrigerator for up to 1 week. Whisk vigorously before serving.

JÍCAMA, CUCUMBER, AND RADISH SALAD
WITH LIME VINAIGRETTE

SERVES 4

1 BUNCH PINK RADISHES (ABOUT 6), THINLY SLICED

1 ENGLISH CUCUMBER, PEELED, CUT IN HALF LENGTHWISE, AND THINLY SLICED

½ SMALL JÍCAMA, PEELED AND SLICED INTO MATCHSTICKS

½ CUP ROUGHLY CHOPPED FRESH CILANTRO

LIME VINAIGRETTE (PAGE 156)

½ TEASPOON CHILE POWDER

KOSHER SALT

This refreshing salad mixes cucumber and peppery radishes with the crispy freshness of jícama. A puckery vinaigrette of fresh lime juice and olive oil and a dusting of chile powder finish the addictive combination.

Combine the radishes, cucumber, and jícama in a large bowl and toss to combine. Add the cilantro to the bowl and drizzle the vinaigrette over the top. Toss gently. Transfer to serving bowls and sprinkle each with a pinch of chile powder and salt to taste.

CORN
AND AVOCADO
SALAD

SERVES 4 TO 6

4 EARS CORN, KERNELS CUT
FROM THE COBS, OR 2 CUPS
FROZEN CORN KERNELS,
DEFROSTED

1/2 MEDIUM RED ONION,
DICED

3 PLUM TOMATOES, DICED

1/2 CUP CHOPPED FRESH
CILANTRO

1 TO 2 JALAPEÑOS, TO
TASTE, SEEDED AND MINCED

1 AVOCADO, CUT INTO
CHUNKS

LEMON VINAIGRETTE
(PAGE 156)

KOSHER SALT

ISABEL'S **tip**

If your corn is young and
tender, there is no need to
cook it. If using corn that is a
little bit tough, boil the
cobs in lightly salted water,
until nearly tender, about
3 minutes, then drain, and
cool completely before slicing
the kernels from the cobs and
combining with the other
ingredients.

This simple summer salad is great as a first
course, as a side—such as for a taco party—or even as a chunky salsa.
It is the perfect backyard barbecue side dish and goes equally well with
chicken, steak, or fish.

Combine the corn, onion, tomatoes, cilantro, and jalapeños in
a medium bowl. Toss to combine. Add the avocado, drizzle
with the dressing, sprinkle with salt to taste, and mix gently.

SPANISH POTATO SALAD

SERVES 6 TO 8

3 POUNDS RUSSET POTATOES, PEELED AND CUT IN HALF

KOSHER SALT

1/2 CUP OLIVE OIL

3 GARLIC CLOVES, MINCED

4 VINE-RIPENED OR PLUM TOMATOES, SLICED

1/2 MEDIUM RED ONION, THINLY SLICED

3 TABLESPOONS DRAINED CAPERS

1/4 CUP FRESH CILANTRO

1 GREEN ONION, WHITE AND GREEN PARTS, SLICED

2 LEMONS, HALVED

FRESHLY GROUND BLACK PEPPER

This brightly flavored potato salad leaves sweet mayonnaisey American versions in the dust. The secret is a warm garlic-infused olive oil that gets poured over the potatoes and a healthy squirt of fresh lemon juice.

············ ❁ ············

Put the potatoes in a large pot and cover with salted water. Bring to a boil and cook until tender, 25 to 30 minutes.

Meanwhile, combine the olive oil and the garlic in a small saucepan. Heat over medium heat, swirling the pan frequently, for about 2 minutes, to infuse the oil with the flavor of the garlic. The garlic will become soft and translucent, but it shouldn't begin to brown. Remove from the heat and cover to keep warm.

Drain the potatoes and set aside to cool. Slice the potatoes into 1/2-inch-thick circles.

Spread out the potato slices on a serving platter. Arrange the tomatoes and onion over the potatoes and then sprinkle the platter with the capers. Garnish with the cilantro leaves and green onion. Drizzle the warm olive oil over the platter. Squeeze the lemon juice over the platter and follow with a sprinkling of salt (but keep in mind that the capers are salty) and pepper.

HEIRLOOM TOMATO AND RED ONION SALAD WITH CILANTRO SAUCE

SERVES 4

3 TABLESPOONS OLIVE OIL

1 LARGE RED ONION, CUT
INTO THICK SLICES

1/2 CUP RED WINE

4 ASSORTED HEIRLOOM
TOMATOES, CUT INTO
THICK SLICES

KOSHER SALT

FRESHLY GROUND BLACK
PEPPER

CILANTRO SAUCE (PAGE 161)

This salad combines the fresh taste of summer heirloom tomatoes with deeply flavorful red onion that has been simmered in red wine. The Cilantro Sauce, which I love on almost anything, gives a cool Latin vibe to this perennially favorite summer salad.

Heat the olive oil in a medium sauté pan over high heat until hot but not smoking. Add the onion slices to the pan and sear them on both sides for about 1 minute. Add the red wine and simmer until the liquid almost disappears, about 3 minutes, turning the onion halfway through. Remove the onion with a slotted spoon and set aside to cool.

Alternate the onion and tomato slices on a serving platter. Sprinkle with salt and pepper and drizzle with the sauce just before serving.

BLUE CHEESE AND WALNUT SALAD WITH CUMIN VINAIGRETTE

SERVES 4

2 HEADS BUTTER LETTUCE, LEAVES TORN INTO BITE-SIZE PIECES

³/₄ CUP CHOPPED WALNUT PIECES

CUMIN VINAIGRETTE (PAGE 156)

6 OUNCES BLUE CHEESE, CRUMBLED OR CUT INTO CHUNKS

¹/₄ CUP CHOPPED FRESH CHIVES

FRESHLY GROUND BLACK PEPPER

This is one of my favorite salads: tender lettuce, crunchy walnuts, and buttery blue cheese, with a Latin twist courtesy of a Cumin Vinaigrette. Add sliced chicken to turn this salad into a meal, or try it with Sofrito Vinaigrette (page 147) to mix things up.

Combine the lettuce leaves and walnuts in a large bowl. Drizzle with the vinaigrette, add the blue cheese and chives, and season with pepper. Toss to combine and serve immediately.

ISABEL'S tip

There's a whole wide world of blue cheeses out there—from French Roquefort to Italian Gorgonzola—each with its own personality. Use your favorite here, or think of this recipe as an opportunity to do some exploring. If you opt for a creamy blue—such as my favorite, American Maytag—it won't crumble, so cut it into chunks using a sharp knife. Do this while the cheese is still cold from the refrigerator.

WATERCRESS, RADICCHIO, ENDIVE, AND AVOCADO SALAD

SERVES 4 TO 6

1 BUNCH WATERCRESS

1 HEAD RADICCHIO, LEAVES TORN INTO BITE-SIZE PIECES

2 HEADS ENDIVE, OUTER LEAVES REMOVED, LEAVES SEPARATED

1 LARGE AVOCADO, CUT INTO CHUNKS

LEMON VINAIGRETTE (PAGE 156)

KOSHER SALT

Avocado tames the bite of watercress, radicchio, and endive in this elegant salad that is crisp and creamy at the same time.

Combine the watercress, radicchio, and endive in a large bowl and toss to combine. Add the avocado, drizzle with the dressing, and season with salt. Gently toss to combine.

SOUPS

I DON'T GO FOR CREAMY, BUTTERY, RICH SOUPS.

With flavorful fresh vegetables, herbs, ginger, and garlic combining to make delicious Tomato-Ginger Soup with Mint Mojo or Corn and Roasted Green Chile Soup, who needs the butter or cream?

Soup has always been a basic meal-in-a-pot for Latin people. In my home, I often make soup as a main course, and my family loves it. Turkey *Albóndigas* in Broth, Cocido, and Abuelita's Chicken and Rice Soup all make filling, delicious main-course meals. And if it's a light lunch you're looking for, a refreshing bowl of Gazpacho will do the trick. Whether you're serving soup as a starter or a main course, nothing says comfort like a pot of homemade soup.

GAZPACHO

SERVES 4 TO 6

ONE 28-OUNCE CAN DICED
TOMATOES, WITH THEIR JUICE

1 CUP TOMATO JUICE

½ CUP OLIVE OIL

4 GARLIC CLOVES, CHOPPED

½ RED BELL PEPPER, CHOPPED

1 LARGE CUCUMBER, PEELED,
SEEDED, AND CHOPPED

1 CUP DRIED BREAD CRUMBS,
PREFERABLY HOMEMADE
(SEE PAGE 68), OR PANKO

1 TABLESPOON KOSHER SALT

1 TEASPOON FRESHLY GROUND
BLACK PEPPER

A Spanish classic, gazpacho has traveled the world.
The bread crumbs are traditional and give the soup body and texture.
It is so quick and easy to make them from scratch, I strongly suggest
it. Top each bowl with a dollop of Avocado-Tomatillo Sauce (page
148) and some diced cucumber.

Combine the tomatoes, tomato juice, olive oil, garlic, bell
pepper, cucumber, bread crumbs, salt, and pepper in a food
processor or blender and purée until well combined while still
retaining some texture. Refrigerate the gazpacho for at least
2 hours or overnight.

Mix well before ladling into chilled bowls.

ROASTED PUMPKIN SOUP

SERVES 6

1 SMALL PUMPKIN (ABOUT
1 POUND), STEMMED AND
HALVED, SEEDS SCOOPED OUT
AND RESERVED

KOSHER SALT

2 TABLESPOONS OLIVE OIL

1 MEDIUM YELLOW
ONION, DICED

3 GARLIC CLOVES, MINCED

2 MEDIUM CARROTS, DICED

2 CELERY STALKS, DICED

1 CUP DRY WHITE WINE

8 CUPS CHICKEN BROTH

2 TABLESPOONS PACKED LIGHT
BROWN SUGAR

1 TABLESPOON GROUND
CUMIN

FRESHLY GROUND BLACK
PEPPER

My first taste of pumpkin wasn't in a pie—it was in my aunt Olga's white beans. Latin cooks have always used pumpkin in all sorts of recipes—everything from fritters to empanadas. Here it takes center stage in a simple soup with a hint of cumin and brown sugar.

Preheat the oven to 350°F.

Place the pumpkin halves, cut side down, on a baking sheet and roast until the skin starts to brown and the flesh feels tender when poked with a knife, about 45 minutes. Remove from the oven and set aside to cool.

While the pumpkin is roasting, rinse the pumpkin seeds and remove any strings from them. Spread out the pumpkin seeds on a clean baking sheet and toast in the oven until lightly golden, about 5 minutes. Sprinkle with salt and set aside to cool.

When cool, peel the skin from the flesh of the pumpkin. Cut the flesh into 2-inch pieces. You should have 1 1/2 to 2 cups roasted pumpkin flesh.

Heat the olive oil in a large heavy-bottomed pot over medium heat. Add the onion and garlic and cook until the onion is soft and translucent, about 4 minutes. Add the carrots and celery and continue to cook until softened, about 5 minutes. Add the white wine and simmer for about 5 minutes, letting the liquid reduce by half. Add the broth, sugar, cumin, and pumpkin flesh. Bring to a simmer and cook for 45 minutes, at which point the vegetables should be very tender.

Purée the soup using an immersion blender or, in batches, in a blender or a food processor. Season the soup with salt and pepper to taste. The soup can be served immediately or covered and refrigerated for up to 3 days. Reheat over medium heat. Ladle into bowls and garnish with the toasted pumpkin seeds.

ISABEL'S tip

This soup can be made with any winter squash, such as butternut or acorn, or even sweet potatoes or yams.

CORN AND ROASTED GREEN CHILE SOUP

SERVES 6 TO 8

3 TABLESPOONS OLIVE OIL

1 MEDIUM YELLOW ONION, DICED

2 MEDIUM CARROTS, DICED

2 CELERY STALKS, DICED

1 CUP DRY WHITE WINE

5 CUPS CHICKEN BROTH

1 LARGE RUSSET POTATO, PEELED AND CUT INTO 1-INCH DICE

4 EARS CORN, KERNELS CUT FROM THE COBS, OR 2 CUPS FROZEN CORN KERNELS, DEFROSTED

ROASTED CHILE VERDE SAUCE (PAGE 146)

KOSHER SALT

This chunky soup is filled with a combination of mild Anaheim chiles, flavorful poblanos, and corn. If you make the chile verde sauce in advance, this soup is ready in no time.

Heat the olive oil in a large heavy-bottomed pot over medium heat. Add the onion and cook until the onion is soft and translucent, about 4 minutes. Add the carrots, celery, and white wine. Bring to a simmer and cook for about 5 minutes, letting the wine reduce by half. Add the chicken broth, potato, corn, and Roasted Chile Verde Sauce. Simmer the soup until the potatoes are tender and easily pierced with the tip of a knife, 20 to 25 minutes.

Season the soup with salt. The soup can be served immediately or stored, covered, in the refrigerator for up to 3 days. Reheat the soup over medium heat.

TOMATO-GINGER SOUP
WITH MINT MOJO

SERVES 6

3 TABLESPOONS OLIVE OIL

1 MEDIUM YELLOW ONION, DICED

4 GARLIC CLOVES, MINCED

3 MEDIUM CARROTS, DICED

2 CELERY STALKS, DICED

¾ CUP ROUGHLY CHOPPED FRESH GINGER

1 CUP DRY WHITE WINE

6 CUPS CHICKEN BROTH

ONE 28-OUNCE CAN DICED TOMATOES, WITH THEIR JUICE

KOSHER SALT

FRESHLY GROUND BLACK PEPPER

MINT MOJO (PAGE 152)

One of my favorite soups to make at home, this is a simple appetizer or lunch. The ginger and Mint Mojo lighten up a traditional tomato soup.

Heat the oil in a large heavy-bottomed pot over medium heat. Add the onion and garlic and cook until the onion is soft and translucent, about 4 minutes. Add the carrots, celery, ginger, and white wine. Simmer for about 10 minutes, or until the wine has nearly completely evaporated. Add the chicken broth and canned tomatoes. Simmer the soup for about 45 minutes, or until the ginger has mellowed and the vegetables are soft.

Using a blender, an immersion blender, or a food processor, purée the soup until smooth, and then season with salt and pepper. Serve immediately or store, covered, in the refrigerator for up to 3 days. Reheat the soup over medium heat. Top with a drizzle of Mint Mojo before serving.

LENTIL SOUP
WITH RED BELL PEPPER, BASIL, AND CHIPOTLE

SERVES 6 TO 8

2 TABLESPOONS OLIVE OIL

1 MEDIUM YELLOW ONION, DICED

4 GARLIC CLOVES, MINCED

1 LARGE RED BELL PEPPER, DICED

1 TABLESPOON CHIPOTLE CHILE POWDER

1 TABLESPOON PAPRIKA

FRESHLY GROUND BLACK PEPPER

1 POUND LENTILS (ABOUT 2½ CUPS), PICKED OVER AND RINSED

4 OUNCES SHIITAKE MUSHROOMS, STEMMED AND SLICED

8 CUPS CHICKEN BROTH

2 BAY LEAVES

¼ CUP CHOPPED FRESH BASIL, PLUS EXTRA FOR GARNISH

KOSHER SALT

This chunky soup has very delicate, subtle flavors that get a little jolt from chipotle chile powder.

Heat the olive oil in a large heavy-bottomed pot over medium-high heat. Add the onion, garlic, and bell pepper, and cook until the onion is soft and translucent, about 3 minutes. Add the chile powder, paprika, and a sprinkling of black pepper, and cook, stirring to coat the vegetables, for about 30 seconds. Add the lentils, mushrooms, chicken broth, bay leaves, and basil. Reduce the heat so the broth simmers, and cook until the lentils are soft, 35 to 40 minutes. Discard the bay leaves.

Using a blender, an immersion blender, or a food processor, purée about half of the soup and return it to the pot. The soup can be stored, covered, in the refrigerator for up to 5 days. Reheat over medium heat. Season with salt then ladle into bowls and garnish with chopped basil.

BUDDHA BOWL

2 GARLIC CLOVES, ROUGHLY CHOPPED

¼ CUP ROUGHLY CHOPPED LEMONGRASS BULB

¼ CUP ROUGHLY CHOPPED FRESH GINGER

2 TABLESPOONS PEANUT OIL

½ MEDIUM YELLOW ONION, CHOPPED

1 MEDIUM CARROT, CHOPPED

1 CELERY STALK, DICED

ONE 14-OUNCE CAN COCONUT MILK

½ CUP WHITE MISO PASTE

1 POUND DRY RICE NOODLES

ISABEL's **tip**

Miso is fermented bean paste. It's highly savory and nutritious and is the base of most Japanese cooking. Made in a few colors from white to red, it's somehow both delicate and hearty at the same time. This recipe calls for white miso paste, which is available in most Asian markets and in the specialty foods section of larger supermarkets.

I've been influenced by the fantastic Asian food of the West Coast and can't help but want to make it my own. This recipe—a mix of rice noodles, coconut milk, and miso paste—has become a signature dish at Isabel's Cantina (folks are always asking me for the recipe) and makes a frequent appearance in my home kitchen, too.

Half of the fun is letting everyone garnish the soup to his liking. A colorful centerpiece would be beautiful bowls of chopped cilantro and mint, green onions, peanuts, and chile flakes.

Combine the garlic, lemongrass, and ginger in a food processor and pulse until finely minced. Set aside.

Heat the oil in a large heavy-bottomed pot over medium heat. Add the onion and cook until soft and translucent, about 4 minutes. Add the carrot and celery and continue cooking until softened, about 4 minutes. Add the garlic mixture and stir to combine. Cook for 2 minutes and then add the coconut milk, miso paste, and 4 cups cold water. Bring to a simmer (be careful not to boil), lower the heat to maintain a simmer, and cook until the miso paste has gently dissolved, 25 to 30 minutes. The broth can be made ahead and stored, covered, in the refrigerator for up to 3 days. Reheat gently.

While the broth is cooking, cook the rice noodles according to package directions.

To serve, place a mound of rice noodles in the center of each soup bowl. Ladle the broth over and serve immediately.

SPANISH CHICKEN AND POTATO SOUP

SERVES 4 TO 6

2 RUSSET POTATOES, PEELED AND CUT INTO 1-INCH PIECES

1 MEDIUM YELLOW ONION, DICED

3 MEDIUM CARROTS, DICED

6 GARLIC CLOVES, CRUSHED AND PEELED

TWO 8-OUNCE BONELESS, SKINLESS CHICKEN BREAST HALVES, CUT INTO 2-INCH PIECES

3/4 CUP OLIVE OIL, PLUS EXTRA FOR SERVING

KOSHER SALT

FRESHLY GROUND BLACK PEPPER

Without broth or cream, this simple, restorative soup gets its body from olive oil and potatoes. This recipe is an adaptation of my Spanish grandmother's recipe, and I always think of it as part of a family meal or something to bring to a friend who is under the weather.

Place the potatoes, onion, carrots, and garlic in a large heavy-bottomed pot. Add about 5 cups cold water to cover the ingredients. Bring to a boil over high heat and then reduce the heat so that the soup simmers. Cook for 15 minutes, add the chicken, and then simmer until the potatoes are tender and the chicken breast is cooked through, about 10 minutes.

Remove from the heat and strain the solids from the broth, reserving both separately. Working in batches, place the solids, including the chicken, in a food processor or blender and pulse the ingredients along with the olive oil and some of the reserved broth to create the consistency you like best. The soup should be thick and rich, but pourable. Season to taste with salt and pepper. The soup can be served immediately or stored, covered, in the refrigerator for up to 2 days. Reheat the soup over medium heat.

Ladle into bowls and drizzle each serving with olive oil.

COCIDO

SERVES 4 TO 6

3 TABLESPOONS OLIVE OIL

1 BEEF SHANK
(ABOUT 1 POUND)

1 MEDIUM YELLOW ONION,
DICED

4 GARLIC CLOVES, MINCED

6 CUPS BEEF BROTH

2 BAY LEAVES

2 EARS CORN, HUSKED
AND EACH CUT INTO
ABOUT 6 WHEELS

2 MEDIUM CARROTS, SLICED

8 OUNCES GREEN BEANS,
ENDS TRIMMED, HALVED

1 MEDIUM ZUCCHINI, DICED

KOSHER SALT

FRESHLY GROUND BLACK
PEPPER

1/2 SMALL RED ONION,
FINELY CHOPPED

2 TABLESPOONS FINELY
CHOPPED FRESH MINT

Traditional cocido, a one-pot meal with a beefy broth, is a staple of Latin cooking. In Spain, Portugal, and Mexico, it's called *cocido* and in Puerto Rico we have a similar version called *sancocho*. Regardless of the name, everyone fights for the corncob wheels that rest in this savory broth. Top each bowl with minced fresh mint and chopped red onion to add a bright finish.

Heat the olive oil in a medium, heavy-bottomed pot over medium-high heat until hot but not smoking. Add the beef shank to the pot. When the meat begins to brown on one side, flip to another side. Brown the meat on all sides, about 8 minutes total. Remove from the pot and set aside on a plate.

Lower the heat under the pot to medium, add the onion and garlic, and cook until the onion has softened, about 3 minutes. Return the beef shank to the pot and add the broth slowly, using a wooden spoon to scrape the caramelized bits from the bottom of the pot.

Add the bay leaves and bring to a simmer over low heat. Cook for 1 hour, then skim any fat or bubbles from the surface and add the corn wheels. Cook for 30 minutes and then add the carrots. Cook until the carrots are tender, 20 to 30 minutes. Add the green beans and zucchini and simmer until they're tender, 5 to 10 minutes.

Recipe continues

Remove the shank from the pot. Scrape all of the meat from the bone and cut the meat into bite-size pieces. Return the meat to the broth, discarding the bone. Discard the bay leaves from the broth. Season to taste with salt and pepper. The soup can be served immediately or stored, covered, in the refrigerator for up to 3 days. Reheat over medium heat.

Serve the soup with a sprinkling of red onion and some mint.

MAIN
COURSES

AS MUCH AS I LOVE TO COOK AND EAT,

I want to spend dinnertime with my family, NOT IN THE KITCHEN, AND I ALSO WANT TO STAY FIT.

So when I decide what's for dinner in my house, I keep all of this in mind. Although steamed fish usually sounds boring to me, when it's red snapper wrapped in foil with tomatoes, ginger, garlic, hearts of palm, and fresh lemon juice, I'm completely on board. This dish has bold flavors and incredible color. Best of all, it's quick and simple to prepare, so it makes the cut in my home as well as in my restaurants.

But you'll see that this chapter also includes recipes like Cumin Panko Chicken, which is breaded and browned in olive oil (and utterly delicious). How can I be talking about healthy eating when there are some fried recipes in this book? For me, the key is balance; I don't eat heavy meals every day or even every week, but every once in a while, I do. I think what is really important is how you pair these heavier foods. When I make Cumin Panko Chicken, I serve it with a steamed or grilled veggie, some steamed brown rice, and a simple, fresh sauce or salsa.

SEA BASS STEAMED IN
BANANA LEAVES 75

**SALMON WITH
PAPAYA-MANGO-
MINT SALSA 76**

**HALIBUT WITH CHERRY
TOMATO—HABANERO SALSA
AND CUCUMBER-CILANTRO
SAUCE 79**

**STEAMED RED SNAPPER
IN FOIL WITH TOMATOES,
HEARTS OF PALM,
AND GINGER 83**

MAHIMAHI WITH JALAPEÑO-
PONZU SAUCE 84

JALAPEÑO SHRIMP 87

**ROASTED CHICKEN WITH
MASHED YUCCA 88**

CHICKEN DIABLO 91

CUMIN PANKO
CHICKEN 93

**GRILLED CHICKEN
BREASTS WITH ROASTED
CHILE VERDE SAUCE 94**

FLANK STEAK WITH
SWEET POTATOES,
CHERRY TOMATOES, AND
GREEN ONIONS 95

**LATIN BURGER WITH
CHIPOTLE-LIME
BARBECUE SAUCE 98**

**GREEN CHILE POSOLE WITH
PORK 100**

LOMO SALTADO 102

ROPA VIEJA 104

CHIPOTLE-MARINATED
GRILLED RIB EYE 106

**NEW YORK STRIP STEAK WITH
BAKED PLANTAIN FRIES 108**

CHAR-GRILLED RACK OF LAMB
WITH CINNAMON
AND CUMIN 111

**CHARBROILED CARNE
ASADA TACOS 112**

**PORK ROAST STUFFED
WITH PINEAPPLE 114**

GRILLED TOFU
WITH AVOCADO
SALSA CRUDA 115

SEA BASS
STEAMED IN
BANANA LEAVES

SERVES 4

10 BANANA LEAVES, SOAKED
IN A BOWL OF HOT WATER
FOR 30 MINUTES

FOUR 6-OUNCE SKINLESS
SEA BASS FILLETS

1 CUP SOY JOY SAUCE
(PAGE 158)

1 CUP BASIC SALSA
(PAGE 141)

ISABEL'S tip

The steaming can be done
in a variety of ways—in a
bamboo steamer set over
some boiling water, or in a
folding vegetable steamer or a
colander set in a large pot of
boiling water. Whatever
device you use, just be sure
that the water isn't touching
the bundles of sea bass and
that the pot is covered with a
tight-fitting lid.

Steaming in banana leaves is a traditional
Latin cooking method, especially in the Yucatán state of Mexico, where
the leaves are used, instead of corn husks, to make tamales. This
steamed sea bass dish is healthy, fun, and makes for a beautiful
presentation.

Firecracker Corn (page 132) makes a great side dish here.

Set up a steamer and bring an inch or two of water to a boil
in it.

Drain the banana leaves (they should be pliable), and pat
them dry with paper towels. Take 2 of the narrowest leaves
and tear long segments from them (these will be used to tie
the wrapped bundles of fish).

Lay 4 of the largest leaves on a clean work surface and place
1 fillet in the center of each leaf. (You may need to overlap
2 leaves.) Top each fillet with 2 tablespoons of the Soy Joy
Sauce and 1 tablespoon of the salsa. Fold the ends up to
enclose the fish. Use the torn pieces to tie each bundle twice.

Place the fish in the steamer and steam for 15 to 17 minutes.
The fish should be opaque throughout and flake easily when
done. Open one packet to check.

While the fish is steaming, heat the remaining Soy Joy Sauce
over low heat.

Serve the fish in their banana leaves in shallow bowls with
bowls of the remaining salsa and warm Soy Joy Sauce to
accompany the dishes.

SALMON
WITH PAPAYA-MANGO-MINT SALSA

SERVES 4

FOUR 6-OUNCE SKINLESS SALMON FILLETS

3 TABLESPOONS CANOLA OIL

½ CUP SOY JOY SAUCE
(PAGE 158)

2 CUPS BABY SPINACH OR ARUGULA

PAPAYA-MANGO-MINT SALSA
(RECIPE FOLLOWS)

ISABEL'S tip

Since salmon is a moist fish that tells you by its color change that it's done, budding cooks will find this an easy dish to master. Look for flesh that is just slightly underdone and reddish on the inside and opaque pink everywhere else. You could certainly use salmon steaks here, but I find the bones make that cut a bit less user-friendly at the table than fillets.

Besides being both healthy and festive, this colorful dish is gorgeous on the plate. Served over a bed of baby spinach or arugula, the fish wilts the greens for a light but delicious dinner.

Heat a large sauté pan, preferably nonstick, over medium-high heat until hot. Rub the salmon fillets on both sides with the oil. Place the salmon in the pan and cook, undisturbed, for at least 3 minutes before turning. Continue to cook until the fish is slightly underdone in the center (use a fork to pull apart the flakes for a peek inside), about 3 minutes, depending on the thickness of the fish. Drizzle the Soy Joy Sauce over the fish, turn the salmon over, and swirl the pan to nicely coat the salmon with the sauce for a minute or two. The fish should be crisp and caramelized on the outside and moist and flaky on the inside.

Divide the spinach among 4 plates and transfer a piece of salmon on top of each plate of greens. Top each piece of salmon with some salsa.

Recipe continues

PAPAYA-MANGO-MINT SALSA

MAKES 2 CUPS

Exotic, flavorful, but oh-so-easy, this mix of fruit, vegetables, and mint adds color and a fresh flavor kick to meats, fish, and, of course, chips. For this salsa, look for fruit that is newly ripe—flavorful but still firm enough to hold its own.

1/2 SMALL PAPAYA, PEELED, SEEDED, AND DICED

1/2 MANGO, PEELED AND DICED

1/2 SMALL RED ONION, DICED

1 JALAPEÑO, SEEDED AND MINCED

1/2 CUP CHOPPED FRESH MINT

Combine the papaya, mango, onion, jalapeño, and mint in a bowl and toss gently to combine. The salsa can be stored, covered, in the refrigerator for up to 3 days.

HALIBUT
WITH CHERRY TOMATO–HABANERO SALSA AND CUCUMBER-CILANTRO SAUCE

SERVES 4

1/2 **PINT CHERRY TOMATOES, HALVED**

1/2 **MEDIUM RED ONION, THINLY SLICED**

1 TO 2 **HABANERO CHILES, TO TASTE, HALVED, SEEDED, AND THINLY SLICED**

1/4 **CUP CHOPPED FRESH MINT**

4 **TABLESPOONS OLIVE OIL**

KOSHER SALT

FOUR 6-**OUNCE SKINLESS HALIBUT FILLETS**

CUCUMBER-CILANTRO SAUCE (RECIPE FOLLOWS)

Halibut is my favorite white fish: It is simple to prepare and the perfect canvas for vibrant flavors. The habaneros, used here in moderation, add just enough heat to make this interesting. The cucumber-cilantro sauce adds a fresh finish to this colorful dish.

Preheat the oven to 350°F.

In a medium bowl, combine the tomatoes, onion, chiles, and mint. Drizzle with 2 tablespoons of the olive oil and sprinkle with 1/2 teaspoon salt. Toss gently to combine.

Lightly season the fillets on both sides with salt. Heat the remaining 2 tablespoons oil in a large sauté pan over medium-high heat. Place the halibut fillets in the hot pan. Brown for about 2 minutes on each side, then transfer to the oven and bake until opaque throughout, 8 to 10 minutes.

Put the halibut fillets on plates and top with a scoop of the tomato salsa. Spoon some of the cucumber-cilantro sauce around the fish. Serve the remaining sauce on the side.

Recipe continues

CUCUMBER-CILANTRO SAUCE

MAKES ABOUT 2 CUPS

1 CUP CHOPPED FRESH CILANTRO

1 CUP DICED, PEELED CUCUMBER

1/2 CUP LEMON JUICE (ABOUT 4 LEMONS)

1/4 CUP OLIVE OIL

1/2 TEASPOON KOSHER SALT

Purée the cilantro, cucumber, lemon juice, olive oil, and salt in a food processor or blender until almost smooth with just a bit of texture. Cover and refrigerate until serving, or for up to 2 days.

STEAMED RED SNAPPER IN FOIL
WITH TOMATOES, HEARTS OF PALM, AND GINGER

SERVES 4

3 PLUM TOMATOES, DICED

½ CUP DRAINED AND SLICED CANNED HEARTS OF PALM

¼ CUP MINCED FRESH GINGER

2 SHALLOTS, THINLY SLICED

2 GARLIC CLOVES, MINCED

3 TABLESPOONS OLIVE OIL

3 TABLESPOONS LEMON JUICE (1 TO 2 LEMONS)

FOUR 6-OUNCE SKINLESS RED SNAPPER FILLETS

KOSHER SALT AND FRESHLY GROUND BLACK PEPPER

FOUR 12-INCH-SQUARE SHEETS OF ALUMINUM FOIL, FOR COOKING THE FISH

CHOPPED FRESH MINT, FOR GARNISH

The chunky salsa that flavors the snapper as it steams has a little bit of everything: Tomatoes, shallots, garlic, olive oil, and hearts of palm give it a bit of delicacy while lemon juice and ginger give it a zing to jolt your palate.

Preheat the oven to 350°F.

In a medium bowl, gently toss together the tomatoes, hearts of palm, ginger, shallots, garlic, olive oil, and lemon juice.

Season the fish with salt and pepper. Lay each piece of fish on a piece of aluminum foil and divide the tomato mixture on top.

Wrap each piece of fish in the foil by bringing up two opposite ends, folding them over once or twice, and then rolling up each of the remaining ends. Be sure to leave some space at the top of the pouch to account for the steam that will be created. Put the foil pouches on a baking sheet and bake for 10 to 12 minutes, until the fish is cooked through and opaque. Carefully open one packet to check.

Place the pouches in bowls, open them carefully (the steam is very hot), and sprinkle with chopped mint before serving.

MAHIMAHI
WITH JALAPEÑO-PONZU SAUCE

SERVES 4

2 TABLESPOONS OLIVE OIL

FOUR 6-OUNCE SKINLESS MAHIMAHI FILLETS

1 TEASPOON KOSHER SALT

1 TEASPOON FRESHLY CRACKED BLACK PEPPER

JALAPEÑO-PONZU SAUCE (RECIPE FOLLOWS)

1 AVOCADO, THINLY SLICED

The jalapeño chiles in the sauce are roasted, which gives a little smokiness to their heat and really shakes up a simple, meaty white fish such as mahimahi.

Preheat the oven to 350°F.

In a large ovenproof sauté pan, heat the olive oil over high heat. Season the mahimahi with the salt and pepper. Place the fillets in the pan. Brown for about 2 minutes before flipping and browning the other side for 2 minutes. Transfer the pan to the oven and bake until the fish is opaque throughout, 6 to 8 minutes.

To serve, generously spoon the jalapeño-ponzu sauce over each piece of fish and top with slices of avocado.

JALAPEÑO-PONZU SAUCE

MAKES ABOUT 1 CUP

Adding jalapeño to traditional Japanese ponzu is a match made in heaven. Bold and delicious, these flavors seem as though they were meant to be together. This also adds zip to a grilled steak.

2 JALAPEÑOS, ROASTED OVER AN OPEN FLAME AND ROUGHLY CHOPPED (SEE PAGE 146)

½ CUP SAKE

⅓ CUP LEMON JUICE (ABOUT 3 LEMONS)

¼ CUP SOY SAUCE

1 TABLESPOON OLIVE OIL

3 TABLESPOONS MINCED FRESH GINGER

2 TABLESPOONS SUGAR

Combine the jalapeños, sake, lemon juice, soy sauce, olive oil, ginger, and sugar in a food processor or blender and pulse until smooth. Transfer to a small saucepan and simmer for about 3 minutes, or until the raw sake taste begins to mellow.

The sauce can be stored, covered, in the refrigerator for up to 1 week. Warm over low heat before using.

JALAPEI
SHRII ..

SERVES 4

3 TABLESPOONS OLIVE OIL

1 MEDIUM RED ONION,
HALVED AND THINLY SLICED

6 GARLIC CLOVES, MINCED

2 JALAPEÑOS, THINLY SLICED
INTO CIRCLES AND SEEDED

1 1/2 CUPS DRY WHITE WINE

1 1/2 POUNDS LARGE SHRIMP,
PEELED AND DEVEINED

1/2 CUP LEMON JUICE
(ABOUT 4 LEMONS)

2 VINE-RIPENED TOMATOES,
ROUGHLY CHOPPED

SEA SALT

This is one of those dishes that you'll make
again and again, not only because it's delicious and satisfying, but
because it also takes practically no time to prepare. For casual Latin
fare, whip up some steamed white rice and Avocado Salsa Cruda
(page 143).

Heat the olive oil in a large sauté pan over medium-low heat.
Add the onion, garlic, and jalapeños. Cook, stirring frequently
so that the garlic doesn't take on any color, until the onion is
soft and translucent, about 2 minutes.

Add the wine and cook for another 2 minutes. Turn the heat
up to medium-high and add the shrimp. When the shrimp are
just beginning to turn pink, add the lemon juice and tomatoes, stirring to combine. Cook until the shrimp are opaque,
another minute or two. Lightly salt the shrimp.

Transfer the shrimp to serving plates, being sure to spoon the
savory sauce from the pan over the shrimp.

ROASTED CHICKEN WITH MASHED YUCCA

SERVES 4

ONE 4-POUND CHICKEN

3 TABLESPOONS KOSHER SALT, PLUS EXTRA FOR SERVING

3 TABLESPOONS OLIVE OIL, PLUS EXTRA FOR SERVING

2 LEMONS, HALVED

ONE 18-OUNCE BAG FROZEN YUCCA

ISABEL'S tip

Frozen yucca, also known as cassava, is available at Latin specialty stores.

Here a simple roasted chicken is served with mashed yucca. Mashed yucca with a drizzle of olive oil and a sprinkle of salt was a favorite of mine as a child. As an adult, I rarely made yucca myself because of the labor involved in peeling the tough brown skin. It was a happy day when I learned that yucca had become available frozen, peeled, and cleaned. Now it is as easy to cook as potatoes.

.... ⚙ ....

Rub the chicken with 2 tablespoons of the salt inside and out. Cover the chicken with plastic wrap and refrigerate overnight.

Preheat the oven to 375°F. Remove the chicken from the refrigerator and pat dry with paper towels. Rub the chicken all over with the 3 tablespoons olive oil. Put the lemon halves in the cavity of the chicken.

Place the chicken in a roasting pan, breast side down (it makes for a juicier chicken), and roast for about 1 1/2 hours, or until the juices run clear when the leg is pierced and the drumsticks move easily when pulled (or the internal temperature of the bird registers 160°F on an instant-read thermometer).

Recipe continues

After the chicken has roasted for nearly an hour, place the frozen yucca in a large pot. Cover with water, add the remaining 1 tablespoon salt, and bring to a boil. Cook the yucca until tender when pierced with a fork, but still holding its shape, about 30 minutes. Drain and set aside in a warm place.

Remove the lemons from the cavity of the chicken and set aside. Cut up the chicken and transfer to warm plates. Skim any fat from the pan juices and drizzle the juices over the chicken. Squeeze the lemons over the chicken. Serve with the yucca, a bottle of olive oil, and some salt. At my house, each person plates his own yucca, smashing it with a fork and then drizzling olive oil on top and sprinkling with salt to taste.

CHICKEN
DIABLO

SERVES 4 TO 6

⅓ **CUP DIJON OR SPICY BROWN MUSTARD**

⅓ **CUP LEMON JUICE (ABOUT 3 LEMONS)**

⅓ **CUP OLIVE OIL**

1½ **TABLESPOONS RED CHILE FLAKES**

3½ **POUNDS BONE-IN CHICKEN PIECES**

This fiery chicken is the perfect dish to make when you haven't much in the fridge but a million other things to do. Marinate it the night before and throw it on the grill when you're ready. It requires very little attention, and its spicy flavor is so addictive, your guests will beg you for the recipe.

This chicken goes really well with Spanish Potato Salad (page 47).

Whisk together the mustard, lemon juice, olive oil, and chile flakes. Put the chicken in a glass baking dish, pour the marinade on top, and turn the pieces to coat. Cover with plastic wrap and refrigerate for at least 2 hours or overnight.

Preheat your grill to high, making sure you have an area for indirect grilling: Either bank the coals to one side or heat only half of a gas grill. Arrange the chicken pieces over the area of the grill without coals, cover the grill, and cook for 10 to 15 minutes per side. The pieces should be crisp with dark grill marks, but with the meat remaining moist. When an instant-read thermometer registers 165° when inserted in the thickest part of the meat (but not touching the bone), remove the pieces. Let rest on a platter for 5 minutes before serving, to allow the juices to redistribute and the meat to finish cooking.

CUMIN PANKO CHICKEN

SERVES 6

6 BONELESS, SKINLESS CHICKEN BREAST HALVES (ABOUT 3 POUNDS)

2 CUPS ALL-PURPOSE FLOUR

3 LARGE EGGS

3 CUPS PANKO

2 TABLESPOONS GROUND CUMIN

1 1/2 TEASPOONS KOSHER SALT

1/4 CUP CANOLA OIL

1 LEMON, CUT INTO WEDGES

ISABEL'S tip

Panko crumbs are larger and flatter than most bread crumbs, get really crispy, and absorb less oil than regular bread crumbs. Panko can be found in Asian markets and sometimes in the specialty foods section of larger supermarkets. Plain dried bread crumbs can be substituted in a pinch.

A little bit of ground cumin and a coating of panko (also known as Japanese bread crumbs) wake up breaded, sautéed chicken breasts. Serve with Oven-Roasted Vegetable Salad with Sofrito Vinaigrette (page 40).

Put the chicken breasts between sheets of plastic wrap or waxed paper and pound with a meat mallet until about 1/2 inch thick.

Put the flour on a plate. Whisk the eggs with 2 tablespoons water in a medium bowl. In a separate bowl, mix the panko with the cumin and salt.

Dredge each piece of chicken first in flour, then in egg, and finally in panko to coat completely.

In a large sauté pan, heat the oil over medium heat. Add the chicken pieces and cook until golden brown and cooked through, about 4 minutes on each side. The key to this recipe is making sure that the chicken cooks on the inside while having a nice golden brown, crispy coating on the outside. If you notice that the outside is cooking too fast and getting too dark, lower the heat.

Arrange the chicken on plates and serve the lemon wedges alongside for squeezing on top.

GRILLED CHICKEN BREASTS
WITH ROASTED CHILE VERDE SAUCE

SERVES 4 TO 6

3 POUNDS BONELESS, SKINLESS CHICKEN BREAST HALVES (ABOUT 6 BREASTS)

¼ CUP OLIVE OIL

KOSHER SALT

2 CUPS ROASTED CHILE VERDE SAUCE (PAGE 146), WARMED

Here's a fresh take on the plain old midweek sautéed chicken breast dinner. Roasted Chile Verde Sauce brings spicy Latin flair to the table, quickly and easily. With a jar of this tasty sauce in the fridge or freezer, you can prepare a school-night meal in minutes. The chicken breasts can be cooked on a hot grill, in a grill pan, or in a countertop electric grill. Rice and beans (see pages 120 to 127) complete the dish.

Preheat your grill to medium-high or heat a grill pan over medium-high heat.

Coat the chicken breasts with the olive oil and season on both sides with salt. Grill the chicken for about 7 minutes per side, or until grill marks appear and the chicken is cooked through.

Transfer the cooked chicken breasts to a platter. Ladle the Roasted Chile Verde Sauce on top and serve hot.

FLANK STEAK
WITH SWEET POTATOES, CHERRY TOMATOES, AND GREEN ONIONS

SERVES 4

¼ CUP PLUS
3 TABLESPOONS OLIVE OIL

¼ CUP RED WINE VINEGAR

1 TEASPOON GROUND
CUMIN

1 TABLESPOON DRIED
OREGANO

KOSHER SALT

1 FLANK STEAK (ABOUT
1½ POUNDS)

2 LARGE SWEET POTATOES,
PEELED AND CUT INTO
1-INCH CUBES

1 PINT CHERRY TOMATOES

2 BUNDLES GREEN ONIONS,
GREEN PARTS ONLY, CUT
INTO 1½-INCH PIECES

FRESHLY GROUND BLACK
PEPPER

½ CUP GUAVA SAUCE
(PAGE 155)

A meat-and-potatoes meal with a twist:

Sweet potatoes and guava bring surprising color and flavor to the table. As always with flank steak, marinate it first to help tenderize, and be sure to sear it over a hot fire or on a grill pan, to brown the outside well while leaving the center pink.

Whisk the ¼ cup oil, the vinegar, cumin, oregano, and ½ teaspoon salt together in a glass baking dish. Add the flank steak, turn so the meat is well coated, and then cover with plastic wrap. Refrigerate for at least 3 hours or overnight.

Place the sweet potatoes in a medium saucepan and cover with salted water. Bring to a boil over medium heat and cook until the sweet potatoes are tender when easily pierced with the tip of a knife but still hold their shape, about 5 minutes. Drain and set aside.

Remove the steak from the refrigerator 15 to 30 minutes before cooking.

Preheat your grill to high or heat a grill pan over medium-high heat.

Place the steak on the hot grill and cook for about 4 minutes, or until browned, before turning. Cook the second side for about 3 minutes for medium-rare. Transfer the flank steak to a cutting board and let it rest while you finish the garnish.

Recipe continues

Heat the 3 tablespoons olive oil in a large sauté pan over medium-high heat until hot but not smoking. Add the sweet potatoes and let them cook, undisturbed, for about 2 minutes before turning them. Cook for about 2 minutes more, or until golden brown and crisp. Add the cherry tomatoes and sauté until they begin to blacken, about 2 minutes. Add the green onions and stir for about 1 minute; they should soften but retain their bright green color. Season with salt and pepper and transfer to a large platter.

Slice the steak against the grain into $1/2$-inch slices. Fan the slices of steak around the vegetables and drizzle the Guava Sauce over the steak. Season with a sprinkling of salt and some pepper.

LATIN BURGER
WITH CHIPOTLE-LIME BARBECUE SAUCE

SERVES 4

3 TABLESPOONS OLIVE OIL

1/2 MEDIUM YELLOW ONION, DICED

4 GARLIC CLOVES, MINCED

1 POUND GROUND TURKEY

1/2 CUP DRIED BREAD CRUMBS

1/2 TEASPOON KOSHER SALT

CHIPOTLE-LIME BARBECUE SAUCE (RECIPE FOLLOWS)

4 WHOLE-WHEAT HAMBURGER BUNS

4 THICK SLICES VINE-RIPENED TOMATO

4 LETTUCE LEAVES

4 RED ONION SLICES

This versatile sauce goes with just about anything hot off the grill. Turkey burgers are a flavorful, healthy alternative to beef. I like to give the burgers one good basting on both sides before grilling. Serve additional sauce on the side for guests to slather on as they wish.

In a small sauté pan, heat 1 tablespoon of the olive oil over medium heat. Add the onion and garlic and cook until the onion is soft and translucent, about 3 minutes. Set aside to cool.

Preheat your grill to medium-high.

Mix the onion mixture with the turkey, bread crumbs, and salt. Form the mixture into 4 burgers, each about 1 1/2 inches thick.

Lightly brush the burgers with the remaining 2 tablespoons olive oil. Pour half of the barbecue sauce into a small bowl and baste the burgers with the sauce. Discard any remaining sauce used for basting. Place the burgers on the grill and cook for 3 to 4 minutes, until browned, before flipping. Cook for 3 to 4 minutes more, until the burgers are cooked through.

When the burgers are nearly done, place the buns on a cooler part of the grill to warm, and toast them for a minute or two.

Serve the burgers with the tomato, lettuce, and red onion sandwiched between the buns. Serve the reserved barbecue sauce in a small bowl on the side.

CHIPOTLE-LIME BARBECUE SAUCE

MAKES 1½ CUPS

6 TO 8 CHIPOTLE CHILES IN ADOBO SAUCE, TO TASTE

½ CUP TOMATO PASTE

½ CUP LIME JUICE (ABOUT 4 LIMES)

2 TABLESPOONS PACKED LIGHT BROWN SUGAR

2 TABLESPOONS BLACKSTRAP MOLASSES

Purée the chipotles, tomato paste, lime juice, sugar, and molasses in a food processor or blender until smooth. The sauce can be stored in the refrigerator for up to 1 week.

GREEN CHILE POSOLE
WITH PORK

SERVES 6

3 TABLESPOONS OLIVE OIL

2½ POUNDS BONELESS PORK SHOULDER, FAT TRIMMED, CUT INTO 2-INCH CHUNKS

KOSHER SALT

FRESHLY GROUND BLACK PEPPER

1 MEDIUM YELLOW ONION, DICED

2 GARLIC CLOVES, MINCED

4 CUPS CHICKEN BROTH

ROASTED CHILE VERDE SAUCE (PAGE 146)

ONE 24-OUNCE CAN HOMINY, DRAINED

ISABEL'S **tip**

I prefer canned hominy to dried because the dried kernels have to be soaked overnight and their cooking time is unpredictable, varying from batch to batch. Canned hominy can be found in Latin markets and some large supermarkets.

Posole is a traditional and hearty Mexican stew made with hominy, dried hulled corn kernels. Serve this hearty stew on its own or with pinto beans, grated Monterey Jack cheese, and some fluffy flour tortillas to scoop everything up in.

Heat the olive oil in a large pot over medium-high heat until hot but not smoking. Dry the cubes of pork with a paper towel and season them with salt and pepper. Working in 3 batches, sear the meat on all sides. Don't move the meat around until it has browned well on each side—about 3 minutes per side. Use tongs to transfer the meat to a platter while you sear the next batch.

When all of the meat has been browned, add the onion and garlic to the pot and stir with a wooden spoon until the onion has softened, about 2 minutes. Add the chicken broth, a little at a time, stirring the browned bits off the bottom of the pan. Return the pork to the pot and bring to a gentle simmer. Lower the heat to maintain the simmer and cook for 1 hour, skimming occasionally.

Add the Chile Verde Sauce and the hominy and continue simmering until the pork is exceptionally tender and the soup is thick and richly flavored, about 1 hour more.

The stew can be served immediately or stored, covered, in the refrigerator for up to 3 days. Reheat over medium heat.

SERVES 6

½ CUP OLIVE OIL, PLUS
EXTRA FOR COATING THE
BAKING SHEETS AND
DRIZZLING

¼ CUP RED WINE VINEGAR

4 GARLIC CLOVES, MINCED

1 NEW YORK STRIP STEAK
(ABOUT 1½ POUNDS),
TRIMMED OF EXCESS FAT

KOSHER SALT

FRESHLY GROUND BLACK
PEPPER

6 LARGE RED POTATOES,
UNPEELED

4 LARGE PLUM TOMATOES,
EACH CUT INTO 6 WEDGES

½ MEDIUM RED ONION,
THINLY SLICED

EASY ESPAÑOLA TOMATO
SAUCE (PAGE 145)

My aunt Candita was married to a man from
Peru. When I was a little girl, I used to watch her making *lomo
saltado,* homemade French fries sautéed with sliced beef (what kid
wouldn't like that!). I lighten up my version by roasting the potatoes in the oven instead of frying them.

To make a marinade for the meat, combine ¼ cup of the
olive oil, the vinegar, and half of the garlic in a small bowl
and whisk together.

Place the steak on a cutting board and, cutting across the
grain of the meat, slice the steak into strips about ¼ inch
thick. Cut the strips into 2-inch pieces. Place the beef in a
glass baking dish, season with salt and pepper, and pour the
marinade over. Toss gently so that all of the meat is coated
with the marinade, and then cover with plastic wrap and
refrigerate for at least 2 hours or overnight.

Cut the potatoes in half and put them in a large pot. Cover
with salted water and bring to a boil. Cook the potatoes until
tender when pierced with a fork but still holding their shape,
about 30 minutes. Drain, and when cool enough to handle,
cut each half into 3 wedges.

Preheat the oven to 350°F.

Lightly coat 2 baking sheets with olive oil. Arrange the potato pieces on one, the tomato wedges on the other. Drizzle each with a little olive oil and season with a sprinkling of salt.

Put both baking sheets in the oven. Roast the tomatoes for about 30 minutes, or until they have a deep red color. Remove from the oven and set aside. Roast the potatoes for about 45 minutes, or until crisp and brown.

Remove the meat from the refrigerator 15 to 30 minutes before cooking.

Heat 2 tablespoons of the olive oil in a large skillet over medium-high heat until hot but not smoking. Working in batches, brown the meat slices. As the meat browns, transfer it to a serving platter while you brown the next batch.

When all of the meat has been browned, add the remaining 2 tablespoons olive oil to the pan. Add the onion and the remaining garlic and sauté until the onion is soft and translucent, about 2 minutes. Return the meat to the pan, add the potatoes and tomatoes, and toss gently to combine and heat through. Season with salt and toss to combine. Transfer to a serving platter.

Serve with a bowl of the tomato sauce, to be spooned over at the table.

ROPA VIEJA

SERVES 4

FOR THE MEAT

1 FLANK STEAK (ABOUT 1½ POUNDS), CUT ACROSS THE GRAIN INTO 4 PIECES

1 MEDIUM YELLOW ONION, HALVED

4 GARLIC CLOVES, CRUSHED AND PEELED

2 BAY LEAVES

½ TEASPOON GROUND CUMIN

A classic of Latin cuisine, *ropa vieja* means "old clothes," and the tender shreds of meat are meant to look like just that. Not the most savory image, I know, but the dish itself is well loved because it is so delicious. Every family has their own way of making this recipe their own. This is mine.

Serve this with steamed white rice and sliced green olives. In my family, we also serve it with a nice glass of red wine.

To cook the meat, combine the steak, onion, garlic, bay leaves, and cumin in a large pot and add enough water to cover completely. Bring to a boil over high heat and then reduce the heat so the water simmers gently. Cook until the meat is very tender and falling apart, 2 to 2½ hours.

Remove the meat from the liquid. Strain the liquid, reserving the broth but discarding the solids. Place the meat in a bowl to cool. When cool enough to handle, shred the meat into small pieces.

FOR THE SAUCE

2 TABLESPOONS OLIVE OIL

1/2 MEDIUM YELLOW ONION, THINLY SLICED

2 GARLIC CLOVES, MINCED

1 RED BELL PEPPER, THINLY SLICED

3/4 CUP DRY WHITE WINE

2 TABLESPOONS TOMATO PASTE

1 CHIPOTLE CHILE IN ADOBO SAUCE, MINCED

1/2 TEASPOON KOSHER SALT

3 GREEN ONIONS, GREEN PARTS ONLY, SLICED

1/2 CUP SLICED GREEN OLIVES (OPTIONAL)

For the sauce, heat the olive oil over medium-high heat. Add the onion, garlic, and bell pepper. Sauté until the bell pepper is tender and the onion is soft and translucent, about 4 minutes. Add the white wine and tomato paste. Stir well and cook for about 5 minutes.

Add the reserved broth, the chipotle, and salt. Continue simmering for another 5 minutes. Add the beef, stir, and cook until the beef is heated through. The *ropa vieja* can be stored, covered in the refrigerator, for up to 3 days. Reheat over medium heat before proceeding. Stir in the green onions and garnish with sliced green olives, if desired, before serving.

CHIPOTLE-MARINATED GRILLED RIB EYE

SERVES 4

½ CUP LIME JUICE (ABOUT 4 LIMES)

3 CHIPOTLE CHILES IN ADOBO SAUCE

3 TABLESPOONS PACKED LIGHT BROWN SUGAR

KOSHER SALT

1 CUP OLIVE OIL

2 RIB EYE STEAKS (ABOUT 16 OUNCES EACH AND 1 INCH THICK)

FRESHLY GROUND BLACK PEPPER

Rib eye is one of my favorite cuts of beef— richly flavorful and tender, this steak on the bone is a cut above. When I serve steak, I want it to be top-notch, and this marinade, with its smoky chipotle kick, never disappoints. Add the Chipotle-Corn Salsa (page 144), a Cucumber Margarita (page 192), and a few friends, and it's a perfect evening. (And since the steaks are pricey, make sure they're good friends!)

Combine the lime juice, chiles, sugar, and 1½ teaspoons salt in a blender. With the blender running, add the olive oil in a steady stream and continue to blend for about 4 minutes to form a frothy emulsion.

Place the steaks in a large glass baking dish and pour half of the chipotle marinade over them. Turn the steaks to coat. Cover with plastic wrap and refrigerate for at least 2 hours or overnight. Refrigerate the remaining marinade separately.

Remove the reserved marinade and the steaks from the refrigerator 15 to 30 minutes before grilling. Preheat your grill to high.

Remove the steaks from the marinade and season them on both sides with salt and pepper. Place the steaks on the grill and cook, undisturbed, for about 5 minutes, before turning them with tongs. Cook for an additional 5 minutes for medium-rare.

Transfer the steaks to a cutting board and let them rest for 5 minutes before cutting each into 2 servings. Serve the reserved chipotle lime sauce marinade to be spooned over the steaks at the table.

NEW YORK STRIP STEAK
WITH BAKED PLANTAIN FRIES

SERVES 4

4 NEW YORK STRIP STEAKS (ABOUT 8 OUNCES EACH)

1 CUP ORANGE-OREGANO DRESSING (PAGE 154)

2 GREEN PLANTAINS, PEELED (SEE PAGE 22)

2 TABLESPOONS CANOLA OIL

KOSHER SALT

FRESHLY GROUND BLACK PEPPER

CHIPOTLE CREAM SAUCE (RECIPE FOLLOWS), OPTIONAL

ISABEL'S **tip**

Chipotle chiles are dried, smoked jalapeños sold in a spicy tomato sauce called adobo. They're sold in ethnic markets, specialty stores, and larger supermarkets and can add a little—or a big—kick to savory dishes.

Steak and pommes frites with a Latin accent, this meal brings fun to a classic. The citrus marinade lends a distinctly Latin flavor, while the baked plantains offer a healthier alternative to traditional French fries. And who needs ketchup? For extra kick, serve with a side of chipotle cream sauce!

Place the steaks in a glass baking dish and pour the Orange-Oregano Dressing over the steaks. Turn the steaks to coat well with the dressing and then cover with plastic wrap and refrigerate for at least 4 hours or overnight.

Remove the steaks from the refrigerator 15 to 30 minutes before grilling.

Preheat the oven to 400°F.

Grate the plantains with the large holes of a box grater. Toss in a medium bowl with 1 tablespoon of the oil and season with salt and pepper. Spread out on a baking sheet coated with the remaining 1 tablespoon oil and bake for 10 to 12 minutes, until crisp and golden brown.

Preheat your grill to high or heat a grill pan over medium-high heat.

Season the steaks on both sides with salt and pepper. Grill the steaks for 4 minutes and then turn. Continue to cook for an additional 4 minutes for medium-rare. Transfer the cooked steaks to serving plates to rest for 5 minutes.

Serve the baked plantain fries alongside the grilled steaks with the chipotle cream sauce, if desired.

CHIPOTLE CREAM SAUCE

MAKES 1¼ CUPS

I mellow out spicy chipotles in this fast, no-cook sauce that can be made ahead of time and refrigerated. Spoon this creamy sauce over tacos, into black beans—I even top burgers with it. And, of course, it is a great dip with tortilla chips. Go skinny if you like by using a low-fat sour cream.

¼ CUP CHIPOTLE CHILES IN ADOBO SAUCE, OR TO TASTE

1 CUP SOUR CREAM OR PLAIN YOGURT

Combine the chiles and sour cream in a food processor or blender and purée until smooth.

The sauce can be stored, covered, in the refrigerator for up to 4 days.

CHAR-GRILLED RACK OF LAMB WITH CINNAMON AND CUMIN

SERVES 4

½ CUP PLUS 1 TABLESPOON OLIVE OIL

3 TABLESPOONS ANCHO CHILE POWDER

3 TABLESPOONS GROUND CINNAMON

3 TABLESPOONS GROUND CORIANDER

3 TABLESPOONS GROUND CUMIN

¼ CUP MINCED FRESH GINGER

6 GARLIC CLOVES, MINCED

ONE 28-OUNCE CAN DICED TOMATOES, WITH THEIR JUICE

KOSHER SALT

¼ CUP HONEY

½ CUP CHOPPED FRESH CILANTRO

2 LAMB RACKS (ABOUT 3 POUNDS TOTAL), SEPARATED INTO CHOPS BY YOUR BUTCHER

MINT MOJO (PAGE 152)

The aromatic marinade is most of the work here (which is to say, not much at all). The smoky flavors of the marinade meld beautifully with the lamb and the bold Mint Mojo. A rack of lamb is a pricey cut of meat, so be sure not to overcook the chops; ideally, they should be a rosy pink in the center.

Heat the 1 tablespoon olive oil in a large sauté pan over medium heat for 30 seconds. Add the chile powder, cinnamon, coriander, and cumin. Swirl and stir the spices until they release their aromas, about 30 seconds. Add the ginger and garlic, stirring for another minute. Add the canned tomatoes and 2 teaspoons salt. Cook the mixture at a low simmer for 30 minutes. Remove from the heat and let the mixture cool completely.

Transfer the tomato mixture to a blender or food processor and purée. Blend in the honey, cilantro, and ½ cup olive oil and process until smooth.

Pour the tomato mixture into a glass baking dish, add the lamb chops, and turn to coat. Cover with plastic wrap and refrigerate for at least 2 hours or, preferably, overnight.

Remove the chops from the refrigerator 15 to 30 minutes before grilling. Preheat your grill to high.

Place the lamb chops on the grill and cook for 2 to 3 minutes per side for medium-rare.

Transfer the lamb chops to a serving platter, drizzling each one with Mint Mojo.

CHARBROILED
CARNE ASADA
TACOS

SERVES 6

¾ **CUP CANOLA OR
PEANUT OIL**

1 **CUP TERIYAKI SAUCE**

6 **GARLIC CLOVES, MINCED**

2 **POUNDS SKIRT STEAK**

**TWELVE 6-INCH CORN OR
FLOUR TORTILLAS**

1 **CUP GRATED MONTEREY
JACK CHEESE**

1½ **CUPS BASIC SALSA**
(PAGE 141)

1½ **CUPS AVOCADO-
TOMATILLO SAUCE** (PAGE 148)

2 **CUPS BLACK BEANS**
(PAGE 120), **OPTIONAL**

When I was first married, our neighbor used
to throw the best taco parties. I begged for the marinade recipe for
the beef, but he wouldn't budge. One night, as I was helping to
clean up, I noticed an empty bottle of teriyaki sauce in his trash. I
would never have guessed his "secret ingredient" and your guests
won't either!

Combine the oil, teriyaki sauce, and garlic in a glass baking
dish. Add the steak, turn to coat, and cover with plastic wrap.
Marinate overnight, turning once or twice.

Remove the steak from the refrigerator 15 to 30 minutes
before cooking.

Preheat your grill to medium-high, or heat a grill pan over
medium-high heat.

Remove the steak from the marinade and discard the marinade. Grill the steak for 4 to 5 minutes per side for medium-rare. The steak should have grill marks and be pink in the center. Let the steak rest on a cutting board for about 5 minutes. Keep the grill on.

Slice the meat thinly, across the grain, then cut into 1-inch pieces.

Heat the tortillas on the grill for 1 minute, turn, and sprinkle each with some grated cheese. When the cheese has melted, remove the tortillas from the grill and fill each with some steak. Serve the tacos, letting the guests add salsa, Avocado-Tomatillo Sauce, and beans to their taste.

PORK ROAST
STUFFED
WITH PINEAPPLE

SERVES 8

¼ CUP OLIVE OIL

5 GARLIC CLOVES, MINCED

ONE 4-POUND BONELESS
PORK LOIN ROAST

1 TABLESPOON
DRIED OREGANO

KOSHER SALT

FRESHLY GROUND
BLACK PEPPER

ONE 20-OUNCE CAN
PINEAPPLE CHUNKS,
DRAINED

GUAVA SAUCE (PAGE 155)

Pork is frequently paired with fruit such as
apples or prunes. The pineapple and guava do it in the Latin style so
well. Oregano and garlic give this dish a savory touch to balance
all the flavors together.

Preheat the oven to 350°F.

Mix together the olive oil and garlic.

Trim away the excess fat from the pork loin and split the loin
in half lengthwise, like a loaf of French bread, but don't cut
all the way through to the other side. Open up the loin and
spread half of the olive oil mixture on top and sprinkle with
1½ teaspoons of the oregano. Season with salt and pepper.
Put the pineapple chunks on the bottom half of the loin and
fold the top half back into place to cover. Tie the roast with
kitchen twine at 1-inch intervals. Spread the remaining olive
oil mixture and the remaining 1½ teaspoons oregano on the
surface of the loin and season with salt and pepper.

Put the roast in a roasting pan and transfer to the oven. Roast
the pork for 30 minutes and then drizzle half of the Guava
Sauce all over the surface of the roast. Roast for about 20
minutes more, or until a meat thermometer inserted in the
center registers 140°F.

Transfer the roast to a cutting board and let rest for 10 minutes. Pour the pan drippings into a glass measuring cup and
remove the fat from the surface with a spoon. Using a sharp
carving knife, cut the pork into ¼-inch-thick slices and serve
with the remaining Guava Sauce and the pan drippings.

GRILLED TOFU
WITH AVOCADO SALSA CRUDA

SERVES 4

1 TABLESPOON GROUND CUMIN

1 TABLESPOON GROUND CHILE POWDER

1 POUND FIRM TOFU, CUT INTO 1-INCH CUBES, DRAINED, AND PATTED DRY WITH PAPER TOWELS

3 TABLESPOONS OLIVE OIL

2 GARLIC CLOVES, MINCED

½ MEDIUM RED ONION, DICED

AVOCADO SALSA CRUDA (PAGE 143)

Who would think of tofu for Latin food?

At my table, I use this combination of flavorful spices to turn anyone into a tofu lover.

Combine the cumin and chile powder in a medium bowl. Add the tofu cubes and toss gently with your hands to coat.

Heat 1 tablespoon of the olive oil in a large sauté pan over medium-high heat. Add the garlic and onion and cook until the onion is soft and translucent, about 2 minutes. Remove with a slotted spoon and set aside.

Add the remaining 2 tablespoons oil to the pan, let it get hot, and then add the tofu to the pan. Cook, turning as needed, to form a crust on all sides of the tofu and heat it through, about 3 minutes. Return the garlic and onion to the pan and stir to combine.

Use a spatula to transfer the tofu to serving plates. Top with the avocado salsa.

RICE, BEANS, AND OTHER SIDES

IF THERE WERE ONLY ONE THING
I COULD CHANGE ABOUT LATIN FOOD,
ABOUT THE WAY WE EAT, IT WOULD BE THIS:
everyone would EAT MORE WHOLE GRAINS.

Not only are they delicious, but whole grains complement Latin cooking so well. If you are new to the whole-grains scene, start with short-grain brown rice and expand from there. Mixing it with barley not only maximizes flavor, but also adds another grain to the table. Quinoa contains more protein than any other grain—in fact, you can think of it as a supergrain. With its subtle couscouslike consistency, Quinoa with Green Olives and Red Onion perfectly combines the saltiness of capers and green olives with the suaveness of olive oil and a little lemon juice to bring everything together.

I admit that if I were to give my teenage sons a mound of steamed brown rice, it probably wouldn't go over so well. But if on top of that were some black beans and an Avocado-Tomatillo Sauce, that would change things. I see toddlers at my restaurants eating heaps of Power Rice (a mixture of brown rice and quinoa) with beans and they love it. These rice and bean recipes are perfect for anyone, anytime. (You'll even find quick recipes using canned beans, for days when planning ahead to soak dried beans just isn't going to happen.) The backbone of Latin cooking, rice and beans also make wonderfully nutritious vegetarian meals.

In this chapter, you'll also find colorful vegetables like Firecracker Corn, Aspirations with Red Bell Pepper and Chile Flakes, and the rock star of complex carbohydrates, sweet potatoes. And, of course, no Latin cookbook would be complete without a traditional recipe for Sweet Plantains.

ARROZ
CON
GANDULES

SERVES 8

**RED BELL PEPPER SOFRITO
(PAGE 147)**

**ONE 15-OUNCE CAN
GANDULES, RINSED AND
DRAINED**

**2 CUPS SHORT-GRAIN
BROWN RICE**

**1 TEASPOON GROUND
CUMIN**

**1 TEASPOON DRIED
OREGANO**

**1 1/2 TABLESPOONS CHILE
POWDER**

KOSHER SALT

ISABEL's **tip**

I love to substitute short-grain brown rice where white rice is normally called for. Brown rice adds texture, flavor, and, most important, fiber, vitamins, and minerals to any meal. Gandules can be found in Spanish markets and in the specialty foods section of larger supermarkets.

I can hardly remember a family gathering without a big pot of arroz con gandules, rice with pigeon peas, a Puerto Rican favorite. My mom, aunts, grandmothers, and dad all had their different versions: Some added pieces of meat to the pot to make it more of a meal; others served it as a side dish to a roast with a simple salad. I know that my grandmother Isabel (looking down from heaven) would like my version with brown rice because she loved reinventing classic recipes herself.

This recipe includes both rice and peas, so it is perfect to serve as the only side along with a main dish.

Heat the sofrito in a medium, heavy-bottomed pot over medium-high heat. Cook, stirring, until fragrant, about 3 minutes. Add the gandules and mix well to combine. Add the rice, cumin, oregano, and chile powder and season with salt. Stir well to combine, and then add 5 cups cold water. Bring to a boil and then lower the heat to maintain a simmer. Cover and cook until the water has been absorbed and the rice is tender, about 1 hour.

Remove from the heat and let stand, covered, for 15 minutes before serving.

BLACK
BEANS

SERVES 6 TO 8;
MAKES ABOUT 8 CUPS

1 POUND DRIED BLACK BEANS, PICKED OVER AND RINSED

2 TABLESPOONS OLIVE OIL

1 MEDIUM SPANISH ONION, DICED

5 GARLIC CLOVES, MINCED

2 TABLESPOONS GROUND CUMIN

2 TABLESPOONS DRIED OREGANO

2 TABLESPOONS CHILE POWDER

2 BAY LEAVES

1 TABLESPOON DRIED SWEET BASIL

KOSHER SALT

A staple in my home and my restaurants, this is my favorite comfort meal, paired with a steaming hot bowl of brown rice. As a meat-free dish that's high in protein, it makes a great vegetarian main course. Served alongside Chicken Diablo (page 91) or Chipotle-Marinated Grilled Rib Eye (page 106), it's the sort of side dish that helps round out a meal. Delicious, nutritious, and easy to make, beans and rice translate perfectly to the busy American lifestyle.

This is the kind of dish I make with leftovers in mind—the beans can be reheated on the stove top or in the microwave. Add shredded Monterey Jack cheese, Basic Salsa (page 141), and avocado slices for fresh flavor and color. A little chopped fresh cilantro sprinkled on top adds a nice touch at the table.

············ ✻ ············

Soak the beans overnight in a large bowl or pot with enough room and water to allow the beans to double in size. Drain the beans in a colander and rinse well.

Heat the olive oil in a large heavy-bottomed pot over medium-high heat. Add the onion and garlic and sauté until the onion is soft and translucent, about 2 minutes. Stir in the cumin, oregano, and chile powder. Stir to combine and simmer for about 1 minute. Add the beans, 8 cups cold water, the bay leaves, and basil. Bring to a boil and then reduce the heat so that the mixture simmers. Cover partially and simmer for about 2 hours, or until the beans are tender. Add water as needed to maintain the water level $1/2$ inch above the beans.

Season with salt and simmer for another 10 to 15 minutes. Remove and discard the bay leaves before serving.

The beans can be stored, covered, in the refrigerator for up to 3 days. Reheat over medium heat.

QUICK **BLACK BEANS**

Sometimes I just don't have time to soak beans overnight and simmer them for hours on the stove. When I haven't got time for dried, I use canned beans, enhanced with my own seasonings. Canned beans are convenient and, best of all, fast; these beans can be on the table in 15 minutes flat.

Prepare Black Beans, decreasing the cumin, chile powder, and oregano to 1 tablespoon each and substituting two 14-ounce cans of black beans, rinsed and drained, and 2 cups cold water for the dried beans and water. Simmer for 5 minutes.

SOFRITO
RED BEANS

SERVES 6 TO 8;
MAKES ABOUT 8 CUPS

1 POUND DRIED RED BEANS,
PICKED OVER AND RINSED

3 CUPS RED BELL PEPPER
SOFRITO (PAGE 147)

1 TABLESPOON ANCHO
CHILE POWDER

1 TABLESPOON GROUND
CUMIN

1 TABLESPOON DRIED
OREGANO

1 TABLESPOON DRIED
SWEET BASIL

2 BAY LEAVES

KOSHER SALT

QUICK SOFRITO
RED BEANS

Prepare Sofrito Red Beans,
substituting two 14-ounce
cans of red beans, rinsed and
drained, and 2 cups cold
water for the dried beans and
water. Decrease the sofrito to
1¹/₂ cups. Simmer for 5
minutes.

Latin cuisine has endless takes on beans, as
varied as Latin cultures themselves. While Cuban cuisine leans
toward black beans, Puerto Rican cooking is partial to red beans.
This recipe holds a special place in my heart because my father
made it for my wedding rehearsal dinner, where he served it with
rice and Sweet Plantains (page 131). It was a very special night
with a very special meal, but you can enjoy it anytime.

Soak the beans overnight in a large pot or bowl with enough
room and water to allow them to double in size. Drain in a
colander and rinse well.

Heat a large, heavy-bottomed pot over medium heat and add
the sofrito. Cook for about 1 minute, or until fragrant. Add
the chile powder, cumin, and oregano. Stir well and continue
cooking for 2 minutes. Add the beans, 8 cups water, the basil,
and bay leaves. Bring to a boil, then reduce the heat so that
the mixture simmers. Cover partially and simmer for about
2 hours, or until the beans are tender. Add water as needed to
maintain the water level ¹/₂ inch above the beans.

Season with salt and simmer for another 10 to 15 minutes.
Remove and discard the bay leaves before serving.

The beans can be stored, covered, in the refrigerator for up to
3 days. Reheat over medium heat.

CHIPOTLE WHITE BEANS

**SERVES 6 TO 8;
MAKES ABOUT 8 CUPS**

**1 POUND DRIED WHITE
BEANS (CANNELLINI, NAVY,
OR ANY SMALL VARIETY),
PICKED OVER AND RINSED**

**3 CUPS RED BELL PEPPER
SOFRITO (PAGE 147)**

**2 TABLESPOONS CHIPOTLE
CHILE POWDER**

KOSHER SALT

QUICK CHIPOTLE WHITE BEANS

Prepare Chipotle White Beans, substituting two 14-ounce cans of white beans, rinsed and drained, and 2 cups cold water for the dried beans and water. Decrease the sofrito to 1½ cups. Simmer for 5 minutes.

The combination of the sofrito with the chipotle chile powder gives these beans a fantastic color and a smoky flavorful bite. White beans are a favorite of my family. If there are any leftovers, they make delicious burritos with pulled chicken.

Soak the beans overnight in a large bowl or pot with enough room and water to allow the beans to double in size. Drain the beans in a colander and rinse well.

In a large, heavy-bottomed pot over medium-high heat, heat the sofrito until it begins to sizzle, about 1 minute. Add the chipotle chile powder and stir for 1 minute. Add the beans and stir well to coat them with the sofrito. Add 8 cups cold water. Bring to a boil, then reduce the heat so that the mixture simmers. Cover partially and simmer for about 2 hours, or until the beans are tender. Add water as needed to maintain the water level ½ inch above the beans.

Season with salt and simmer for another 10 to 15 minutes.

The beans can be stored, covered, in the refrigerator for up to 3 days. Reheat over medium heat.

BROWN RICE

2 TABLESPOONS OLIVE OIL

2 CUPS SHORT-GRAIN
BROWN RICE

1/2 TEASPOON KOSHER SALT

POWER RICE

Prepare Brown Rice, substituting 1/2 cup quinoa, well rinsed and drained, and 1 cup pearl barley for 1 1/2 cups of the brown rice.

BROWN RICE WITH BARLEY

Prepare Brown Rice, substituting 1 cup pearl barley for 1 cup of the brown rice.

Rice is the staple for more than half the world's population, yet many home cooks these days are intimidated by the range of varieties and cooking methods. If you are a frequent rice-eater, you may want to look into a rice cooker. I use one at home and in the restaurants. While it does occupy valuable counter space, it is the most foolproof way to make perfect rice.

However, making stove-top rice is simple when you have the correct proportion of water to rice. Follow these recipes and you'll be set, as long as you don't forget about the pot on the stove! I like to start rice by sautéing it in a little oil. This toasts the rice, giving it a little extra flavor, and prevents the grains from clumping, but is a completely optional step.

Here is a basic recipe for brown rice, my favorite, as well as two great additional whole-grain variations.

Heat the olive oil in a medium pot over medium heat. Stir in the rice and sauté for 2 to 3 minutes. Add 4 cups cold water and the salt to the pot and bring to a boil. Reduce the heat to low and simmer, covered, until the rice is tender but not mushy and has absorbed all of the water, about 40 minutes.

Remove from the heat and let stand, covered, for 5 to 10 minutes. Fluff with a fork and serve.

WHITE
RICE

SERVES 8;
MAKES ABOUT 6 CUPS

2 TABLESPOONS CANOLA
OR PEANUT OIL

2 CUPS LONG-GRAIN
WHITE RICE

$1/2$ TEASPOON KOSHER SALT

COCONUT RICE

Prepare White Rice, decreasing the water to $3^1/2$ cups and adding $1/2$ cup canned coconut milk with the water. Before serving, top with $1/2$ cup toasted shredded sweetened dried coconut (see page 20 for instructions on toasting coconut).

I normally prefer brown rice to white—both for taste and health reasons—but sometimes nothing but traditional white rice will do, such as in Abuelita's Chicken and Rice Soup (page 65). White rice is also the base of a fantastic variation with toasted coconut (below) that is great for taming spicy foods.

Heat the oil in a medium pot over medium heat. Add the rice and sauté until well coated, 2 to 3 minutes. Add 4 cups cold water and the salt and bring to a boil. Reduce the heat to low and simmer, covered, for about 25 minutes, or until the rice has absorbed all of the liquid and is tender but not mushy.

Remove from the heat and let stand, covered, for 5 to 10 minutes before serving. Fluff with a fork and serve.

QUINOA
WITH GREEN OLIVES
AND RED ONION

SERVES 4 TO 6

1 CUP QUINOA, WELL RINSED AND DRAINED

1/2 TEASPOON KOSHER SALT

1/2 TEASPOON FRESHLY GROUND BLACK PEPPER

5 TABLESPOONS OLIVE OIL

1/2 MEDIUM RED ONION, DICED

1/2 CUP DICED RED BELL PEPPER

3/4 CUP GREEN OLIVES, HALVED AND PITTED

3 TABLESPOONS LEMON JUICE (1 TO 2 LEMONS)

1 TEASPOON GROUND CUMIN

1/2 CUP CHOPPED FRESH CILANTRO

Quinoa (pronounced keen-wah) is a grain as ancient as the Incas themselves, who held this crop to be sacred.

For more than six thousand years, it has been an important complete food, called "the mother of all grains" for its superhigh protein content. I always have cooked quinoa on hand to add to salads and soups, or to serve as a side dish. Here it serves as the perfect backdrop for the bold flavors of olive and red onion.

Place the quinoa in a medium saucepan and cover with 2 cups cold water. Bring to a boil over high heat and then reduce the heat so that the mixture simmers. Cover and cook until the water has been absorbed and the quinoa is tender, 10 to 15 minutes. Remove from the heat, stir in the salt and pepper, and set aside.

Heat 3 tablespoons of the olive oil over medium heat. Add the onion and sauté until soft and translucent, about 4 minutes, and then add the bell pepper. Continue cooking until the bell pepper has softened, about 3 minutes. Add the olives, stirring well to combine, and cook for 1 minute more.

Stir the sautéed vegetables into the quinoa. Add the lemon juice, the remaining 2 tablespoons olive oil, the cumin, and cilantro. Toss well to combine. Serve the quinoa warm, at room temperature, or cold. The quinoa can be stored, covered, in the refrigerator for up to 3 days.

PAN-GRILLED SWEET POTATOES AND YAMS

SERVES 4 TO 6

1 LARGE SWEET POTATO (ABOUT 12 OUNCES)

1 LARGE YAM (ABOUT 12 OUNCES)

KOSHER SALT

3 TABLESPOONS OLIVE OIL

FRESHLY GROUND BLACK PEPPER

ISABEL'S tip

Try to find sweet potatoes and yams that are about the same size so that they will cook at the same rate and be done at the same time.

We serve this simple side at the restaurants as a nutritious but flavorful alternative to buttery potato dishes. People ask for the recipe and are always surprised to find how easy it is to make one of the healthiest carbs around! Serve sweet potatoes and yams with Char-Grilled Rack of Lamb with Cinnamon and Cumin (page 111) or substitute this dish for yucca and serve with the roasted chicken on page 88.

Rinse the sweet potato and yam. Place in a large pot and cover with salted water. Bring to a boil over high heat. Cook until the sweet potato and yam are tender (pierce them with the tip of a paring knife) but still hold their shape, about 45 minutes. Drain and let cool slightly. Peel and slice each one into 1/2-inch slices.

Heat the olive oil in a large sauté pan over medium-high heat. When the oil is hot but not smoking, place the sweet potato and yam in the pan. Cook for 2 minutes, turn, and cook for 2 minutes more. The yam and sweet potato should be crispy and caramelized on both sides. Transfer to a serving dish, season with salt and pepper, and serve immediately.

SWEET
PLANTAINS

SERVES 6 TO 8

2 LARGE RIPE PLANTAINS

**ABOUT 1½ CUPS CANOLA
OR PEANUT OIL, FOR FRYING**

KOSHER SALT

The skins of plantains let you know how sweet they will be and this classic recipe calls for the sweetest, ripest ones, those with yellow skins and black spots. Unlike green plantains, these don't need to be soaked before cooking.

To peel the plantains, cut off the ends of each plantain and then use a paring knife to peel the skin off in strips from top to bottom. Cut each plantain on the diagonal into ½-inch-thick slices.

Pour enough oil into a large deep-sided sauté pan to come ½ inch up the sides, and heat over medium-high heat until small bubbles begin to form on the bottom of the pan. (If you have a frying thermometer and want to use it, the temperature you are looking for is 350°F.) Place half of the plantain slices in the hot oil (they should sizzle but not cause the oil to spatter; lower or raise the heat accordingly). Fry for 1 minute before turning the slices over with tongs or a slotted spoon. Cook for about 1½ minutes more, or until golden brown.

Transfer to a paper-towel-lined tray to drain. Sprinkle with salt. Repeat with the remaining plantain slices. Serve hot.

FIRECRACKER
CORN

SERVES 4

3 TABLESPOONS OLIVE OIL

3 RED JALAPEÑOS, THINLY SLICED INTO CIRCLES, SEEDS DISCARDED

4 EARS CORN, KERNELS CUT FROM THE COBS, OR 2 CUPS FROZEN CORN KERNELS, DEFROSTED

KOSHER SALT

This lively, simple side dish is made of a few ingredients in a couple of minutes. Use great summer corn when it's available, frozen organic when it isn't. Red jalapeños are the same as green jalapeños, except they are left on the vine longer to ripen. When cooked, they are a bit sweeter (not spicier) and their color brightens the dish.

Heat the oil in a medium sauté pan over medium-high heat. Add the jalapeños and cook until softened, about 3 minutes. Add the corn and sauté for a minute or two, until the corn is tender and hot. Season with salt and transfer to a serving bowl. The corn can be stored, covered in the refrigerator, for up to 1 day. Serve hot or at room temperature.

SAUTÉED COLLARD GREENS WITH GOLDEN BEETS

SERVES 4 TO 6

1 POUND GOLDEN BEETS

5 TABLESPOONS OLIVE OIL

½ MEDIUM RED ONION, DICED

3 GARLIC CLOVES, MINCED

1 BUNCH COLLARD GREENS, CENTER RIB REMOVED, LEAVES THINLY SLICED

KOSHER SALT

FRESHLY GROUND BLACK PEPPER

Collard greens are popular in Brazil and other parts of Latin America, where they are typically served with black beans and rice. I serve them with golden beets because I love the contrast in colors, and I certainly love the taste of this so-good-for-you side dish.

Bring a medium pot of salted water to a boil. Rinse the beets and cut off the leafy tops, leaving 1 inch of the stem. Submerge the beets in the boiling water and cook until the tip of a knife easily pierces them, 20 to 40 minutes, depending on the size of the beets. Drain and rinse under cool water. When the beets are cool enough to handle, rub the skins off under running water. Cut into ¼-inch slices. Set aside.

Heat 2 tablespoons of the olive oil in a large sauté pan over medium heat. When the oil is hot, add the onion and garlic and cook until the onion is soft and translucent, about 3 minutes. Add the collard greens and cook, stirring as needed, until the leaves have wilted but still retain their bright green color, about 3 minutes.

Pile the collard greens on a serving platter and surround with the beet slices. Drizzle the remaining 3 tablespoons olive oil over the top and season with a sprinkling of salt and pepper.

ISABEL'S **tip**

To thinly slice the collards (or any leafy green), cut out the stems, stack a few of the leaves together, roll them up lengthwise, and then cut them with a sharp straight-bladed knife. Slicing the collards this way is not only easy, but helps them cook quickly in this recipe.

ASPIRATIONS
WITH RED BELL PEPPER AND CHILE FLAKES

SERVES 4 TO 6

4 TABLESPOONS OLIVE OIL

2 BUNCHES ASPIRATIONS (ABOUT 1 POUND), ENDS TRIMMED

1 RED BELL PEPPER, CUT INTO ¼-INCH STRIPS

2 TEASPOONS RED CHILE FLAKES

½ TEASPOON KOSHER SALT

Also known as broccolini, aspirations are a cross between broccoli and Chinese kale. They make a great match with red bell pepper and chile flakes in this colorful side dish. If you can't find aspirations, you can substitute broccoli florets or even broccoli rabe.

Heat the oil in a large sauté pan over medium heat until hot but not smoking. Add the aspirations and toss to coat with the oil. After they begin to wilt, 2 to 3 minutes, add the bell pepper and, stirring frequently, cook until it has softened and slightly caramelized, about 5 minutes.

Add the chile flakes and salt and stir to combine. Serve hot or at room temperature.

SALSAS,
SAUCES,
AND
MARINADES

I AM A SAUCE PERSON.

FOR THE MOST PART,
I prefer a
SIMPLE MEAL
WITH A SAUCE THAT REALLY
PACKS IN THE FLAVOR.

In this chapter (and attached to individual dishes throughout this book), you'll find sauces that will not only perfectly complement many of the dishes in this book, but also allow you to shake up your own repertoire. These sauces are versatile and can work in countless combinations. Mix and match, and remember: There are very few dishes that don't taste better when topped with bright green, herbaceous Cilantro Sauce, if you ask me.

One of my favorite ways to maximize flavor is by layering marinades and sauces in one dish. Salmon with Papaya-Mango-Mint Salsa (page 76) is a perfect example: First the salmon is drizzled with Soy Joy Sauce (a gingery soy sauce, page 158) and then it is topped off with a fantastic fruit salsa. The result is a riot of flavor and an incredibly healthful meal. Get creative, and you'll be rewarded with bold, fresh dishes that you can make in a flash!

BASIC
SALSA

MAKES 3 CUPS

**ONE 28-OUNCE CAN
PLUM TOMATOES, WITH
THEIR JUICE**

**4 YELLOW CHILES OR
2 JALAPEÑOS, STEMMED**

**½ MEDIUM YELLOW ONION,
ROUGHLY CHOPPED**

**2 GARLIC CLOVES, CRUSHED
AND PEELED**

**1 CUP FRESH CILANTRO,
TOUGH STEM ENDS REMOVED**

GRATED ZEST OF 1 LIME

KOSHER SALT

Salsa is not just for tortilla chips and tacos.
With no fat and lots of flavor, this salsa is one of the easiest ways
I know to turn a simple grilled piece of chicken or fish and even
scrambled eggs into something more vibrant.

Combine the tomatoes, the chiles, onion, garlic, cilantro, lime
zest, and salt to taste in the work bowl of a food processor or
in a blender and pulse until the mixture is well combined but
still chunky.

Store the salsa, covered, in the refrigerator for up to 3 days.
Bring to room temperature before serving.

AVOCADO
SALSA CRUDA

MAKES 1½ CUPS

4 PLUM TOMATOES, CUT INTO MEDIUM DICE

½ CUP CHOPPED FRESH CILANTRO

1 AVOCADO, DICED

3 TABLESPOONS SOY SAUCE

Fresh with the creaminess of avocado and tomatoes and with the saltiness coming from soy, this sauce is addictive. I crave it almost every day. I think you will, too. Serve this simple chunky salsa as is or as a topping for grilled tofu, fish, or meat, or rice and beans.

Gently combine the tomatoes, cilantro, and avocado in a small bowl. Pour the soy sauce over the salsa. Serve immediately.

CHIPOTLE-CORN SALSA

MAKES 3 CUPS

4 EARS CORN, KERNELS CUT
FROM THE COBS, OR 2 CUPS
FROZEN CORN KERNELS,
DEFROSTED (SEE ISABEL'S TIP,
PAGE 46)

½ MEDIUM RED ONION,
DICED

½ RED BELL PEPPER, DICED

2 CHIPOTLE CHILES IN
ADOBO SAUCE, MINCED

½ CUP LIME JUICE
(ABOUT 4 LIMES)

¼ CUP ORANGE JUICE
(ABOUT 1 ORANGE)

2 TABLESPOONS PACKED
LIGHT BROWN SUGAR

½ CUP ROUGHLY CHOPPED
FRESH CILANTRO

½ TEASPOON KOSHER SALT

Have you noticed how good frozen corn has gotten? I have. While nothing beats fresh summer corn, I'm thrilled to have organic frozen corn kernels available all year round. Good thing, because this salsa, with the smoky heat of chipotle chiles in adobo, is terrific all year round, too. Serve it with chips, of course, or alongside roasted or grilled meats and fish, or rice and beans. I adore it with the Chipotle-Marinated Grilled Rib Eye (page 106).

Combine the corn kernels, onion, bell pepper, chipotles, lime juice, orange juice, sugar, cilantro, and salt in a medium bowl and gently toss together. Serve immediately or store, covered, in the refrigerator for up to 2 days.

EASY
ESPAÑOLA
TOMATO SAUCE

MAKES 2 CUPS

ONE 15-OUNCE CAN DICED TOMATOES, WITH THEIR JUICE

3 GARLIC CLOVES, MINCED

¼ CUP EXTRA-VIRGIN OLIVE OIL

KOSHER SALT

FRESHLY GROUND BLACK PEPPER

This simple no-cook condiment is like a Spanish version of homemade ketchup—and you'll find as many uses for it as ketchup. I serve this with Easy Turkey Empanadas (page 31) and Lomo Saltado (page 102). Keep some on hand, and you'll discover new ways to serve it everyday.

Team this up with Cilantro Sauce (page 161) for an excellent pairing of flavors.

Combine the tomatoes, garlic, olive oil, and salt and pepper to taste in a blender and purée until smooth. Use immediately or store, covered, in the refrigerator for up to 3 days.

ROASTED
CHILE VERDE
SAUCE

MAKES ABOUT 5 CUPS

3 TABLESPOONS OLIVE OIL

1 MEDIUM YELLOW ONION, DICED

5 GARLIC CLOVES, MINCED

4 ANAHEIM CHILES, ROASTED AND CHOPPED (SEE BELOW)

2 POBLANO CHILES, ROASTED AND CHOPPED (SEE BELOW)

1 POUND TOMATILLOS, ROASTED AND PURÉED (SEE PAGE 148)

3 PLUM TOMATOES, DICED

KOSHER SALT

ISABEL's **tip**

This sauce is easy to make but has a few steps. Begin by fire-roasting your chiles and making a tomatillo purée. This can be done in advance, and the roasted chiles and tomatillos can be refrigerated for up to 3 days.

There are countless ways to use this versatile sauce. Besides using this in Grilled Chicken Breasts with Roasted Chile Verde Sauce (page 94), Corn and Roasted Green Chile Soup (page 58), and Green Chile Posole with Pork (page 100), I'll also serve this with tortilla chips.

Heat the oil in a deep, straight-sided sauté pan over medium heat. Add the onion and garlic, and cook until the onion is soft and translucent, about 3 minutes. Add the chiles, the tomatillo purée, and the tomatoes. Bring to a simmer and cook for about 5 minutes to allow the flavors to blend.

Add 1 cup cold water and gently simmer over low heat for about 30 minutes, or until thickened. Season with salt to taste. Serve hot.

The sauce can be stored, covered, in the refrigerator for up to 3 days. Reheat over medium heat before serving.

TO FIRE-ROAST CHILES: *Place the chiles over an open flame (such as on a gas stove top) and roast, turning as needed, until the skins turn a blistery black. Place them in a bowl and cover with plastic wrap for 10 to 15 minutes. The heat will help steam the skins off. Use a paper towel to rub the charred skins from the flesh. Slice each chile in half, remove and discard the seeds, and roughly chop. Remember not to touch your face or your eyes while working with chiles and to wash your hands thoroughly after touching them.*

RED BELL PEPPER SOFRITO

MAKES 1½ CUPS

½ CUP OLIVE OIL

1 RED BELL PEPPER, CUT INTO MEDIUM DICE

1 LARGE YELLOW ONION, CUT INTO MEDIUM DICE

4 GARLIC CLOVES, CRUSHED AND PEELED

ISABEL's tip

I like to make sofrito in big batches—you can easily double or triple this recipe and divide it among resealable plastic bags, and freeze it for future use.

SOFRITO VINAIGRETTE

MAKES 1¼ CUPS

Whisk together ½ cup Red Bell Pepper Sofrito, ½ cup extra-virgin olive oil, ¼ cup balsamic vinegar, 2 teaspoons packed light brown sugar, 2 teaspoons minced fresh rosemary, and salt and freshly ground black pepper to taste.

Use immediately or store, covered, in the refrigerator for up to 3 days. Whisk before using.

Sofrito is a base of olive oil, bell pepper, onion, and garlic used in Latin cooking to add body, depth, and fabulous flavor to almost every dish. I learned how to make this sofrito from my aunt Eddie and while I might occasionally add a little hot chile pepper or dried oregano, this recipe remains the base, the starting point of so many wonderful Latin dishes.

Heat the olive oil in a medium sauté pan over medium heat. Add the bell pepper, onion, and garlic and sauté until the onion is soft and translucent but not brown, about 5 minutes. Transfer the contents of the pan to a food processor and pulse to form a rough paste. (Alternatively, you can let the mixture cool and then finely chop the mixture by hand.)

The sofrito can be stored, covered, in the refrigerator for up to 3 days or frozen for up to 2 months. Defrost before using.

ROASTED
TOMATILLO
SAUCE

MAKES ABOUT 2 CUPS

8 OUNCES TOMATILLOS, HUSKS REMOVED, RINSED

1 JALAPEÑO, STEMMED

1 GARLIC CLOVE, PEELED

1 TEASPOON KOSHER SALT

AVOCADO-TOMATILLO SAUCE

MAKES ABOUT 3 CUPS

Add 1 diced avocado and ¼ cup fresh cilantro to the food processor along with the tomatillos, and pulse until combined but still chunky. Serve immediately or store, covered, in the refrigerator for up to 2 days.

Tomatillos are small green tomatoes with a papery husk that is easily peeled away. They have a fruity and zesty flavor that makes for an appealing alternative to red salsas. As an ancient Mexican ingredient, tomatillos are a culinary cornerstone of Latin cooking. As a modern American salsa, this is a deliciously fat-free way to boost the flavor of scrambled eggs, grilled fish, or even your favorite tortilla chips.

Preheat the oven to 375°F.

Place the tomatillos, jalapeño, and garlic on a rimmed baking sheet. Transfer to the oven and roast until the tomatillos begin to crack, 20 to 30 minutes.

Transfer the contents of the baking sheet (including any juice from the tomatillos) to the work bowl of a food processor and purée until smooth. Season with the salt and set aside to cool.

The sauce can be made ahead and stored, covered, in the refrigerator for up to 5 days or frozen for up to 3 months. Defrost before serving.

AVOCADO-TOMATILLO SAUCE

ROASTED TOMATILLO SAUCE

CILANTRO-GARLIC MOJO

MAKES 1 CUP

2 CUPS ROUGHLY CHOPPED FRESH CILANTRO

4 GARLIC CLOVES, CHOPPED

¼ CUP EXTRA-VIRGIN OLIVE OIL

¼ CUP LEMON JUICE (ABOUT 2 LEMONS)

ISABEL's tip

My grandmother would grind the ingredients together in a big wooden mortar. I'm a fan of modern conveniences, so I like to flick the switch on a mini-chop food processor, and—zip—it's done.

Mojo (pronounced mo-ho, not mo-joe) is a Latin do-everything condiment. A mojo is made of garlic, herbs, olive oil, and citrus, and there's no end to the variations. Spoon it over fish, grilled chicken, or meat.

Combine the cilantro, garlic, olive oil, and lemon juice in the work bowl of a food processor and pulse to a pestolike consistency.

Use immediately or store, covered, in the refrigerator for up to 2 days. Mix well before using.

MINT
MOJO

MAKES 1 CUP

¹/₂ **CUP FRESH CILANTRO**

¹/₂ **CUP FRESH MINT**

2 **GARLIC CLOVES, PEELED**

3 **TABLESPOONS
EXTRA-VIRGIN OLIVE OIL**

1 ¹/₂ **TABLESPOONS FRESH
LEMON JUICE**

1 ¹/₂ **TEASPOONS SUGAR**

Like Cilantro-Garlic Mojo (page 151), this paste is a fragrant mix of herbs and spices that adds bold flavor to meat, fish, and poultry. Unlike sauces with butter or cream, mojos are a much lighter alternative. This mojo is a fresh and a natural partner for Char-Grilled Rack of Lamb with Cinnamon and Cumin (page 111).

············ ✿ ············

Combine the cilantro, mint, garlic, olive oil, lemon juice, and sugar in the work bowl of a food processor and pulse to a pestolike consistency.

Use immediately or store, covered, in the refrigerator for up to 2 days. Mix well before using.

BALSAMIC
DRESSING

MAKES 1½ CUPS

½ CUP BALSAMIC VINEGAR

1 TABLESPOON PACKED
LIGHT BROWN SUGAR

1 TABLESPOON MINCED
FRESH ROSEMARY

2 GARLIC CLOVES, MINCED

1 CUP EXTRA-VIRGIN
OLIVE OIL

ISABEL's tip

When making dressings, you
can whisk the ingredients
together or, as I often do, use
the blender. The blender both
whips and aerates the
dressing, making it smooth,
cohesive, and frothy—a
perfect emulsion.

This fragrant (and slightly sweet) balsamic
dressing is perfectly balanced for any salad. I particularly love it over
organic lettuces or with grilled chicken.

Using a blender, an immersion blender, or a bowl and whisk,
blend together the vinegar, sugar, rosemary, and garlic. Drizzle in the olive oil in a fine stream and blend to combine.

Use immediately or store, covered, in the refrigerator for up
to 3 days. Whisk before using.

ORANGE-OREGANO DRESSING

MAKES 1½ CUPS

½ CUP RED WINE VINEGAR

¼ CUP ORANGE JUICE
(ABOUT 1 ORANGE)

1 TEASPOON DRIED
OREGANO

1 TEASPOON RED CHILE
FLAKES

1 TABLESPOON PACKED
LIGHT BROWN SUGAR

½ TEASPOON KOSHER SALT

½ CUP EXTRA-VIRGIN
OLIVE OIL

Layers of flavors make this a particularly delicious salad dressing—a must with Orange and Fennel Salad (page 39). It reinforces the orange flavor of the salad and adds just a bit of heat and color to the flavors; it's also great over greens and roasted vegetables—even with poached fish or meats.

In a small bowl, whisk together the vinegar, orange juice, oregano, chile flakes, sugar, and salt. Drizzle the olive oil in a slow stream while whisking the ingredients together.

Use immediately or store, covered, in the refrigerator for up to 2 days. Whisk before using.

GUAVA SAUCE

MAKES ABOUT 1 CUP

⅓ CUP CUBED GUAVA PASTE

1 GARLIC CLOVE, MINCED

2 TABLESPOONS OLIVE OIL

2 TABLESPOONS DRY WHITE WINE

½ TEASPOON KOSHER SALT

Guava is everywhere in the Caribbean and grows domestically in California. Its unforgettable flavor and vibrant rusty red color are central to Latin cooking. Guava paste is a concentrated form of the fruit and can be found in Latin markets and in the specialty foods section of larger supermarkets. Use this sauce to drizzle over roasted meats or a piece of grilled fish.

Combine the guava paste and the garlic with ⅔ cup cold water in a small saucepan over medium heat. When the guava paste has dissolved, add the olive oil, white wine, and salt. Simmer for 2 minutes, whisking to combine the ingredients. Let cool completely.

Store the Guava Sauce, covered, in the refrigerator for up to 1 week. Whisk with a tablespoon or two of water before serving to bring it to the desired consistency, if needed.

LEMON
VINAIGRETTE

MAKES ABOUT ½ CUPS

¼ CUP LEMON JUICE
(ABOUT 2 LEMONS)

½ TEASPOON KOSHER SALT

⅓ CUP EXTRA-VIRGIN
OLIVE OIL

LIME VINAIGRETTE

Substitute lime juice for the
lemon juice in Lemon
Vinaigrette.

CUMIN
VINAIGRETTE

Add ½ teaspoon ground
cumin to Lemon Vinaigrette.

This hardly seems like a recipe, but every time
I serve it, people ask me how to make it. So here it is! This is great
with a green salad or a composed salad.

············ ✻ ············

In a small bowl, whisk together the lemon juice and salt. Drizzle the olive oil in a fine stream into the bowl while whisking to combine.

Use immediately or store, covered, in the refrigerator for up to 3 days. Whisk before using.

LEMON
VINAIGRETTE

ORANGE-
OREGANO
DRESSING
(PAGE 154)

CUMIN
VINAIGRETTE

SOY JOY SAUCE

MAKES 1½ CUPS

¼ **CUP PLUS**
2 TABLESPOONS SOY SAUCE

2 TABLESPOONS DARK
SESAME OIL

2 TABLESPOONS HONEY

2 TABLESPOONS MINCED
FRESH GINGER

1 GARLIC CLOVE, MINCED

½ **CUP FRESH CILANTRO**

½ **TEASPOON CHILE FLAKES**

This is my million-and-one-uses sauce: It's an excellent marinade for meat, fish, and poultry; a seasoning for stir-fries; and a great sauce for grilling sliced mushrooms for an unforgettable side dish. This sauce showcases how well Latin and Asian food can influence each other in creative ways, and I've made it a part of my "East meets West Coast" Latin cooking.

Combine the soy sauce, sesame oil, honey, ginger, garlic, cilantro, and chile flakes in a food processor or blender. Add ¼ cup plus 2 tablespoons cold water and purée until smooth.

The sauce can be stored, covered, in the refrigerator for up to 1 week.

SWEET SOY
SAUCE

MAKES 1 CUP

1 CUP SOY SAUCE

1 CUP SUGAR

Think of this thick, syrupy sauce as you would a balsamic vinegar reduction: It drizzles beautifully over fish and meats to add a little salty-sweet kick of flavor.

Combine the soy sauce and the sugar in a medium saucepan. Bring to a boil over medium-high heat, then lower the heat and stir occasionally until the sugar has completely dissolved. Simmer until the sauce has thickened, about 20 minutes. (The sauce will continue to thicken as it cools, so don't let it get too thick on the stove.) Let cool completely.

The sauce can be stored, covered, in the refrigerator for up to 1 month.

CILANTRO
SAUCE

MAKES 1 CUP

½ CUP EXTRA-VIRGIN
OLIVE OIL

¼ CUP RED WINE VINEGAR

1 GARLIC CLOVE, MINCED

½ CUP ROUGHLY CHOPPED
FRESH CILANTRO

¼ TEASPOON KOSHER SALT

CILANTRO–LIME
SAUCE

Prepare Cilantro Sauce, substituting lime juice for the red wine vinegar.

This is one of my most called upon sauces, used for everything from salads to meats. Besides the distinctive flavor of cilantro, this adds brilliant color to the plate.

Combine the olive oil, vinegar, garlic, cilantro, and salt in a food processor and purée until nearly smooth. The sauce can be stored, covered, in the refrigerator for up to 2 days.

DESSERTS

COCONUT FLAN.

CROISSANT BREAD PUDDING
with Mexican Chocolate and Almonds.

RICE PUDDING
with Cinnamon, Star Anise, and Mango.

RICH, CREAMY, CHOCOLATY

LATIN DESSERTS ARE MY WEAKNESS.

Whenever I've tried to totally eliminate something I love from my diet, like Flourless Chocolate-Ginger Cake, all I've done is sit around all day and think about it. To me, that's worse than if I'd just satisfied the craving and had a slice! So now I don't fight my sweet tooth. If you eat healthful fresh food most of the time, a few bites of something decadent can be simply heavenly. And that is what this chapter is really about: treating yourself to sweet, warm, indulgent, real desserts.

That isn't to say that there aren't some great healthful recipes in here, because there are. Tropical Fruit with Tequila-Honey Sauce and Coconut Tofu Sauce with Fresh Fruit, for example, are perfect for topping off a slightly heavier meal.

BANANAS
WITH VANILLA ICE CREAM AND RUM

SERVES 4

½ CUP (1 STICK) UNSALTED BUTTER

¾ CUP PACKED DARK BROWN SUGAR

3 RIPE BUT FIRM BANANAS, PEELED AND SLICED ¼ INCH THICK ON THE DIAGONAL

2 TABLESPOONS FRESH ORANGE JUICE

¼ CUP DARK RUM

4 SCOOPS VANILLA ICE CREAM

½ CUP CHOPPED PEANUTS

This is a take on the classic bananas Foster. While the bananas make a fantastic, simple dessert, you can also serve them—without the ice cream—alongside pancakes or French toast for a great addition to a brunch menu.

Combine the butter and brown sugar in a large sauté pan over medium heat. Swirl the pan until the butter melts and the mixture thickens and caramelizes, about 3 minutes.

Add the bananas to the pan, and stir to coat with the caramel. Cook for about 2 minutes, or until the bananas have softened. Stir in the orange juice until it is completely incorporated, about 20 seconds. Add the rum and simmer for 2 minutes to cook away the raw alcohol taste.

Spoon the bananas into 4 bowls, top each with a scoop of vanilla ice cream, and then sprinkle with the chopped peanuts. Serve immediately.

COCONUT
FLAN

**MAKES ONE 9-INCH
FLAN; SERVES 8**

1 CUP SUGAR

**ONE 8-OUNCE PACKAGE
CREAM CHEESE, SOFTENED**

PINCH OF SALT

**ONE 14-OUNCE CAN
COCONUT MILK**

**ONE 14-OUNCE CAN
SWEETENED CONDENSED
MILK**

**6 LARGE EGGS, LIGHTLY
BEATEN**

ISABEL'S **tip**

The smooth caramel top of a traditional coconut flan can be an intimidating feat to first-timers. While it does look and taste great, you can certainly skip it and just concentrate on the creamy sweet flan. But practice makes perfect when it comes to caramel, so I encourage you to give the caramel a whirl. Just remember, hot syrup is extremely hot, so be careful, and don't let the kids help with that step.

The creamy texture and tropical coconut flavor make this flan irresistible. Cream cheese makes for a firmer texture, tangier taste, and a somehow even more delicious custard.

Center a rack in the oven and preheat the oven to 325°F.

Place a 9-inch cake pan next to the stove. Place the sugar in a small, heavy saucepan and drizzle $1/3$ cup water evenly over the top. Place the pan over medium heat and swirl the pan to mix the sugar and water. Continue swirling until completely dissolved. When a clear syrup has formed, cover the pot and cook for 2 minutes at a boil. Uncover, and swirl the pot again, cooking until the syrup turns a dark amber color. Carefully pour the bubbling syrup into the cake pan, tilting the dish to spread the caramel evenly.

In the bowl of an electric mixer or working by hand in a large bowl with a wooden spoon, combine the cream cheese and salt and beat until smooth. Stir in the coconut milk and then the condensed milk to make a smooth batter. Add the eggs and mix on low speed until just combined. Pour into the cake pan.

Place the cake pan in a larger baking dish filled with enough water to reach halfway up the pan, about 1 inch. Bake for about 60 minutes, or until the mixture is set in the center and jiggles only slightly when the pan is tapped lightly. Remove from the oven, let cool to room temperature, and then chill for at least 4 hours or overnight.

To serve, place the flan in a large dish of hot water for 3 to 4 minutes to loosen the caramel from the pan. Remove the cake pan from the water and dry the bottom of the pan with a dish towel. Run a knife around the edges of the pan and then invert it onto a serving plate. The caramel will run down the sides of the flan as you remove the cake pan. Serve immediately.

STRAWBERRY-MANGO
COBBLER

**MAKES ONE 9-INCH
COBBLER; SERVES 8**

**2¹/₂ CUPS PLUS
2 TABLESPOONS
ALL-PURPOSE FLOUR**

¹/₄ TEASPOON SALT

1¹/₂ CUPS SUGAR

**1 CUP (2 STICKS) UNSALTED
BUTTER, SOFTENED**

2 LARGE EGGS

**1 PINT STRAWBERRIES,
HULLED AND CUT INTO
QUARTERS**

**1 LARGE MANGO,
PEELED AND CUT INTO
1-INCH CHUNKS**

This cobbler is made of two layers of fruit and two layers of dough. Less precise in its assembly than a pie, it's fun and fast to put together. The food processor makes foolproof dough every time. Strawberries and mangoes are my favorites, but use whatever fruit combination you wish.

Serve with a little vanilla ice cream, of course.

Preheat the oven to 350°F.

Pulse the 2¹/₂ cups flour, the salt, 1 cup of the sugar, and the butter in a food processor or electric mixer until incorporated but still slightly crumbly. (Alternatively, you can combine the ingredients by hand in a bowl using a wooden spoon.) Add the eggs and pulse to combine; do not overmix. The dough will have a smoother consistency now. Divide the dough into 2 equal pieces. (If desired, the dough can be wrapped in plastic wrap and refrigerated overnight. Bring to room temperature before proceeding.)

In a medium bowl, toss the strawberries and mango with the remaining ¹/₂ cup sugar and the 2 tablespoons flour.

In a 9-inch pie plate, use your fingers to lightly press 1 piece of dough into a circle to cover the bottom of the plate. Spread three-quarters of the fruit mixture over the dough. Press the remaining piece of dough into a 9-inch circle on a lightly floured cutting board and layer the dough over the fruit. Top with the remaining fruit mixture.

Bake the cobbler until the crusts are golden brown and the fruit is bubbling, about 55 minutes.

Let the cobbler cool at least briefly before serving. Serve warm or at room temperature.

COCONUT
TOFU SAUCE
WITH FRESH FRUIT

SERVES 6

ONE 14-OUNCE CAN COCONUT MILK

ONE 12-OUNCE BOX SILKEN TOFU, DRAINED

1/4 CUP SUGAR

1/2 CUP SHREDDED SWEETENED DRIED COCONUT, TOASTED (SEE PAGE 20)

4 CUPS CUT-UP FRUIT, SUCH AS HULLED AND QUARTERED STRAWBERRIES, ORANGE SEGMENTS, KIWI SLICES, PINEAPPLE CHUNKS, OR MANGO CHUNKS

With no dairy or flour, this light dessert is perfect for a hot summer day. Exotic, and actually good for you, the sauce also happens to be delicious, which is really the main reason to make it.

Combine the coconut milk, tofu, sugar, and 1/4 cup of the toasted coconut in a blender or food processor. Purée until smooth. Refrigerate until needed or for up to 2 days.

Arrange your selection of fruit on a platter. Pour the chilled coconut tofu into a small serving bowl and sprinkle with the remaining 1/4 cup toasted coconut. Place in the center of the fruit platter and serve immediately.

CROISSANT BREAD PUDDING WITH MEXICAN CHOCOLATE AND ALMONDS

SERVES 6 TO 8

BUTTER, FOR THE PAN

3 LARGE EGGS

1 1/2 CUPS HALF-AND-HALF

2 TABLESPOONS PACKED
LIGHT BROWN SUGAR

4 TO 6 CROISSANTS,
ENOUGH TO FILL A 9-INCH
PIE PLATE, SPLIT IN HALF AS
FOR A SANDWICH

MEXICAN CHOCOLATE
(RECIPE FOLLOWS)

1 CUP SLICED ALMONDS

Warm and delicious, bread pudding is always a treat, even more so when it's made with flaky croissants and cinnamony Mexican chocolate. Plan on serving this warm from the oven, if possible.

With croissant sizes varying from bakery to bakery, you'll have to see how many fit into your pie pan depending on how big or small your croissants are.

Preheat the oven to 350°F. Butter a 9-inch pie plate and set aside.

Combine the eggs, half-and-half, and brown sugar in a large bowl. Whisk to combine. Press the sliced croissants into the egg mixture and soak for 3 minutes, turning once or twice. They should absorb the egg mixture but not to the point of falling apart. Fit the bottom half of each croissant into the buttered pie plate, sliced side down.

Sprinkle 1 cup of the Mexican chocolate over the croissants and then 1/2 cup of the almonds. Layer the remaining halves of the croissants, sliced side down again, on top. Sprinkle the remaining 1/2 cup Mexican chocolate and the remaining 1/2 cup almonds over the top.

Bake the bread pudding until puffy and dry on top but still moist inside, 45 to 60 minutes. Remove from the oven and let cool slightly before cutting and serving. Serve warm, at room temperature, or chilled. The bread pudding can be stored, covered, in the refrigerator for up to 4 days.

Recipe continues

MEXICAN CHOCOLATE

MAKES 1 1/2 CUPS

Chocolate has always been an integral part of Mexican culture, with cocoa beans having been used as currency; buried alongside leaders; and, of course, made into drinks, moles, and sweets. Both the Mayans and the Aztecs flavored their chocolate—sometimes with honey, herbs, cinnamon, and even chiles. Besides bread pudding, this can be used for Mexican Hot Chocolate (page 199). Make ahead and store until needed.

1 CUP SEMISWEET CHOCOLATE CHIPS

1/2 CUP SUGAR

1 TABLESPOON GROUND CINNAMON

Combine the chocolate chips, sugar, and cinnamon in a food processor and pulse until finely ground. Store in a cool, dry place in an airtight container.

FLOURLESS CHOCOLATE-GINGER CAKE

MAKES ONE 10-INCH CAKE; SERVES 10 TO 12

2 1/2 CUPS SEMISWEET CHOCOLATE CHIPS (ABOUT 15 OUNCES)

1 1/2 CUPS (3 STICKS) UNSALTED BUTTER, PLUS EXTRA FOR THE PAN

2 TABLESPOONS MINCED FRESH GINGER

1 TABLESPOON GROUND GINGER

12 LARGE EGG YOLKS

3/4 CUP GRANULATED SUGAR, PLUS EXTRA FOR THE PAN

6 LARGE EGG WHITES

COCOA POWDER OR CONFECTIONERS' SUGAR, FOR DUSTING

I make this rich, chocolaty cake frequently, as it is always in demand by my sons! If you're not a ginger fan, simply omit it. Fresh berries or Raspberry Puree (page 180) accompany this cake very well.

Preheat the oven to 325°F.

Butter and dust with granulated sugar a 10-inch springform pan.

Melt the chocolate chips and butter in a microwavable bowl in the microwave or in the top of a double boiler. Add the fresh and ground gingers and whisk until thoroughly combined with no lumps. Set aside to cool.

With an electric mixer, beat the egg yolks with 6 tablespoons of the sugar until the mixture is pale and thick, about 4 minutes.

With clean beaters and in a clean bowl, whip the egg whites and the remaining 6 tablespoons sugar until the mixture holds soft peaks.

Use a rubber spatula to scrape the beaten egg yolks into the cooled melted chocolate and fold to combine. Fold the beaten egg whites into the chocolate mixture. When well combined, pour into the prepared pan.

Bake for 30 to 40 minutes, until the cake top is puffed up and dry and a toothpick inserted in the center comes out with moist crumbs stuck to it. Remove from the oven and let cool at least slightly. The cake will collapse a little as it cools.

The cake can be served warm, at room temperature, or cold. Run the tip of a knife around the edge of the cake and open the springform pan. Dust with cocoa before cutting into pieces. Well wrapped, the cake can be stored for up to 1 day at room temperature or 4 days in the refrigerator. The cake also freezes well for up to 1 month. Defrost before serving.

RICE PUDDING
WITH CINNAMON, STAR ANISE, AND MANGO

SERVES 4

1 CUP MEDIUM- OR SHORT-GRAIN RICE

1/4 TEASPOON SALT

5 CUPS WHOLE MILK

1 CUP SWEETENED CONDENSED MILK

3 WHOLE STAR ANISE

1 CINNAMON STICK

1 VANILLA BEAN, SPLIT LENGTHWISE

1 MANGO, PEELED AND DICED

ISABEL'S tip

I find that a good-quality Chinese or Japanese short- or medium-grain rice works best and can be found at Asian markets or in larger supermarkets.

Rice pudding takes on an exotic edge when simmered with star anise and cinnamon and served with diced mango. It's just enough of a twist to make it interesting to adults but still comforting to the kids.

Bring 2 cups cold water to a boil in a medium saucepan. Add the rice and salt, stir once, and reduce the heat so that the mixture simmers. When the rice has absorbed most of the water, about 20 minutes, add the whole milk, sweetened condensed milk, star anise, cinnamon stick, and vanilla bean. Stir thoroughly to combine.

Simmer the pudding over medium heat, stirring occasionally, until it begins to thicken, 15 to 20 minutes. Reduce the heat to medium-low and begin stirring regularly to avoid scorching as the pudding continues to thicken to an oatmeal-like consistency. This can take 30 to 45 minutes. Remove from the heat and let cool to room temperature.

Remove the star anise, cinnamon stick, and vanilla bean. Refrigerate the rice pudding until cold, at least 1 hour or, covered, for up to 3 days.

Serve the chilled rice pudding in individual bowls and top with the mango.

TROPICAL FRUIT
WITH TEQUILA-HONEY SAUCE

SERVES 6

1 ½ CUPS CUBED HONEYDEW

1 ½ CUPS CUBED CANTALOUPE

1 MANGO, PEELED AND DICED

2 KIWIS, PEELED AND DICED

¼ CUP HONEY

½ CUP PREMIUM GOLD TEQUILA

¼ CUP FINELY CHOPPED FRESH MINT

A light, fun dessert for adults, this fruit salad has more than a hint of tequila. If you've got a crowd for Sunday brunch, this is a must.

Toss the honeydew, cantaloupe, mango, and kiwis in a medium bowl and then divide among 6 martini glasses. Refrigerate until ready to serve or for up to 1 day.

Combine the honey and tequila and whisk until thoroughly blended. Refrigerate until ready to serve.

Remove the martini glasses from the refrigerator. Whisk the mint into the sauce and then drizzle the sauce over each portion.

CHURROS
WITH RASPBERRY PURÉE

FOR THE RASPBERRY PURÉE

3 CUPS OR ONE 12-OUNCE BAG FROZEN RASPBERRIES

½ CUP SUGAR

FOR THE CHURROS

½ CUP (1 STICK) UNSALTED BUTTER

½ TEASPOON SALT

1 CUP ALL-PURPOSE FLOUR

3 LARGE EGGS

ABOUT 3 CUPS CANOLA OR PEANUT OIL, FOR FRYING

ABOUT 1 CUP SUGAR

Churros are a delicious Latin treat that I lighten up slightly by serving them with a raspberry purée. Wonderful for dessert, they're also a great way to start the weekend—just add coffee and the morning paper.

To make the raspberry purée, combine the raspberries and sugar in a medium saucepan. Heat over medium heat, stirring occasionally, until the berries have broken down, 15 to 20 minutes.

Transfer the mixture to a food processor or blender and purée until smooth. Pass through a strainer to remove the seeds. Refrigerate, covered, until ready to serve or for up to 1 week.

To make the churros, combine the butter and salt with 1 cup cold water in a medium saucepan. Bring to a boil over medium-high heat. Remove from the heat. Add the flour all at once and mix quickly with a heavy wooden spoon until combined. Let the dough cool slightly for 3 to 4 minutes. Stir in the eggs, one at a time, making sure each egg is fully combined before adding the next one. When the dough is finished, it should be smooth and shiny.

Put the dough into a pastry bag fitted with a large star tip. On a parchment-lined baking sheet, pipe 3-inch lines of dough. (This can be done up to 1 day ahead of time. Wrap with plastic wrap and store in the refrigerator. Take the dough out of the refrigerator and let it come to room temperature before frying.)

Heat about 2 inches of oil in a large straight-sided sauté pan over medium-high heat until small bubbles form at the bottom of the pan. (If you have a frying thermometer and want to use it, the temperature you are looking for is 350°F.) Working in batches, place the lines of dough in the pan. Fry for 1 to 2 minutes before turning and cooking for another minute or two, until golden brown. Transfer to a paper-towel-lined tray to drain.

Place the sugar in a brown paper bag, add some churros, and shake lightly to coat with sugar. Serve immediately with the raspberry purée for dipping.

DRINKS

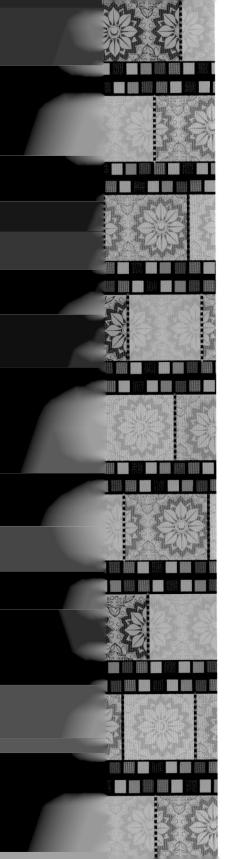

LATIN AMERICA'S BOLD COLORFUL FOODS ARE BEST MATCHED WITH EQUALLY FULL-BODIED DRINKS.

Infusing cucumber and mint into chilled water creates an easy, refreshing summertime drink, while making jalapeño vodka for a fiery martini spices up any cocktail hour. From *aperitivos* and accompaniments to a meal, to drinks to sip and enjoy just on their own in a quiet moment, you'll find recipes here perfect for every occasion.

POMEGRANATE
MARTINI

MAKES 1 MARTINI

1 LIME, HALVED

SUGAR

2 OUNCES CHILLED VODKA

2 OUNCES CHILLED POMEGRANATE JUICE

ICE CUBES

POMEGRANATE SEEDS, FOR GARNISH (OPTIONAL)

The vibrant color and delicate taste of this
martini belie its potency, so watch out!

Rub the rim of a chilled martini glass with the cut lime and then dip in sugar to coat the rim.

Squeeze 1 tablespoon juice from the lime and combine in a cocktail shaker with the vodka and pomegranate juice. Add ice cubes to the shaker and shake gently. Strain into the prepared glass and garnish with pomegranate seeds. Serve immediately.

RASPBERRY-LIME
AGUA FRESCA

MAKES ABOUT 12 CUPS

**3 CUPS OR ONE 12-OUNCE
BAG FROZEN RASPBERRIES**

½ CUP SUGAR

**½ CUP LIME JUICE
(ABOUT 4 LIMES)**

ICE CUBES

FRESH MINT SPRIGS

LIME WEDGES

This is a delicious everyday drink that the whole family can enjoy. It's refreshing and festive and a great alternative to sodas. *Aguas frescas* are made with many types of fruits and enjoyed throughout Latin America. If desired, you can spike this for adults with white rum or tequila.

Place the raspberries, sugar, and lime juice in a blender along with 2 cups cold water. Purée, and then pour the mixture into a large pitcher. Stir in 6 cups cold water. Refrigerate for at least 1 hour and up to 2 hours.

Stir well before serving. Pour the *agua fresca* over ice and garnish with mint sprigs and a lime wedge.

MAKES ABOUT 8 CUPS

1 GREEN APPLE, CORED AND
CUT INTO 1-INCH CHUNKS

5 STRAWBERRIES, HULLED
AND THINLY SLICED

½ CUP CANNED PINEAPPLE
CHUNKS WITH ½ CUP JUICE

2 LIMES, THINLY SLICED

ONE 750-ML. BOTTLE DRY
WHITE WINE

¼ CUP TRIPLE SEC

1 CUP ORANGE JUICE
(ABOUT 4 ORANGES)

½ CUP LEMONADE

ICE CUBES

White sangria isn't seen as frequently as red,

which might be why I like it so much. As a summer party drink, this is without equal. Make it well ahead of time, giving the fruit and liquor some time to mingle.

Combine the apple, strawberries, pineapple, limes, wine, triple sec, orange juice, and lemonade in a large pitcher and chill for at least 2 hours or up to 2 days. Serve the sangria in glasses filled with ice, being sure to include a selection of the fruit in each glass.

JALAPEÑO **MARTINI**

MAKES 1 MARTINI

2 TABLESPOONS JALAPEÑO VODKA (RECIPE FOLLOWS)

2 TABLESPOONS VERMOUTH

1 TABLESPOON FRESH LIME JUICE

1 TABLESPOON FRESH LEMON JUICE

8 ICE CUBES

With its peppery jolt, this martini is for the spicy-lovers and daring drinkers among us. Lots of fun to serve and to drink, the Jalapeño Martini requires a little advance vodka preparation and a bit of jalapeño roasting, but it's worth it!

In a cocktail shaker, combine the vodka, vermouth, lime juice, and lemon juice. Add the ice cubes to the shaker and shake gently. Strain into a chilled martini glass and serve immediately.

JALAPEÑO VODKA

**MAKES ONE
750-ML. BOTTLE**

ONE 750-ML. BOTTLE
PREMIUM VODKA

2 RED JALAPEÑOS, ROASTED
(SEE PAGE 146) AND COOLED

2 GREEN JALAPEÑOS, ROASTED
(SEE PAGE 146) AND COOLED

If you are using a new bottle of vodka, pour out a little of the vodka to make room for the jalapeños. Halve the jalapeños lengthwise and drop them into the bottle. Screw on the cap and store in the freezer. The jalapeño vodka will be ready to use the next day but will keep nearly indefinitely in the freezer.

CUCUMBER
MARGARITA

MAKES 4 MARGARITAS

1/4 CUP PLUS
2 TABLESPOONS FRESH
LIME JUICE

1/4 CUP PLUS
2 TABLESPOONS PREMIUM
GOLD TEQUILA

1/4 CUP TRIPLE SEC

1 CUCUMBER, PEELED,
SEEDED, AND DICED

3 CUPS ICE CUBES

These are unbelievably refreshing and good looking, too, destined to become your trademark party drink. I'm guessing that almost everyone has watched a bartender salt the rims of margarita glasses, but if you haven't, invert the glass into a dish of lime juice and then into a dish of kosher salt. Put the glasses in the freezer until you're ready to pour, then rev up your blender, and don't forget to garnish the margarita with a few slices of cool cucumber.

Combine the lime juice, tequila, triple sec, and cucumber in a blender. Add the ice and blend to a slushy consistency.

Pour into chilled glasses with salted rims and enjoy immediately.

STAR
TEA

MAKES 4 CUPS

4 CHAMOMILE TEA BAGS

2 CINNAMON STICKS

4 WHOLE STAR ANISE

2 TABLESPOONS HONEY

JUICE OF 1 ORANGE

JUICE OF 1 LEMON

I love a caffeine-free tea for afternoons and evenings but find most of them a little lackluster. I started glamming up chamomile tea with spices and now make this tea that lets me sleep at night but doesn't bore me. It's aromatic and delicious cold or hot. I think it's as sexy as chamomile tea can get.

Bring 4 cups cold water to a boil and pour into a 32-ounce heatproof container. Add the tea bags, cinnamon sticks, star anise, and honey. Let the ingredients steep for 3 minutes. Add the orange and lemon juices and stir to blend. The tea can be served immediately or chilled for iced tea.

NUEVO
COQUITO

MAKES ABOUT 7 CUPS

TWO 14-OUNCE CANS COCONUT MILK

ONE 14-OUNCE CAN SWEETENED CONDENSED MILK

1 1/2 CUPS PREMIUM WHITE RUM

ICE CUBES

Like eggnog, a *coquito* is a traditional Puerto Rican drink served during the holidays. I serve it over ice to lighten it up just a bit.

Combine the coconut milk, condensed milk, and rum in a food processor or, working in batches, a blender. Purée until frothy. Transfer to a pitcher and serve in tall glasses over ice.

CUCUMBER-
MINT WATER

MAKES ABOUT 8 CUPS

**1 ENGLISH CUCUMBER,
PEELED AND CUT INTO
HALF-MOONS**

**¼ CUP CHOPPED
FRESH MINT**

ICE CUBES

I will admit—I'm a California girl and as such
I'm a spa fan. Since I can't spend as much time as I'd like being
cleansed and coddled, I might spend a whole day with this
rejuvenating water, bringing a little spa state of mind to my
workday. You'd be surprised how energizing it can be. It's also
great with spicy foods. Rather than buy flavored waters, why
not make your own?

Combine the cucumber and mint in a pitcher with 8 cups
cold water and chill for at least 1 hour or up to 1 day.

Serve over ice if you like.

MEXICAN
HOT CHOCOLATE

MAKES 1 CUP

2 TABLESPOONS MEXICAN CHOCOLATE (PAGE 172)

1 CUP MILK

Mexican hot chocolate is a drink and dessert all wrapped into one. With canela (cinnamon) and just a hint of sweetness, this warm and comforting drink is great with churros (page 180) in the morning, or just on its own practically anytime.

Combine the chocolate and milk in a small saucepan. Heat over medium heat until steaming hot, stirring constantly so the milk is almost foamy. Serve hot.

BREAKFASTS

THE MOST POPULAR BREAKFASTS AT MY RESTAURANTS are two extremes: THE POWER BREAKFAST (egg whites, brown rice, and steamed vegetables with salsa) AND, ON THE OTHER END, sweet and eggy COCONUT FRENCH TOAST WITH MANGO.

You couldn't get a much wider spread.

There are people clearly on each end of the spectrum who never venture beyond their favorites. And then there are people like me who tend to stay most of the time somewhere in the middle but occasionally drift over to either side. I think we are happier than either of those two extremes!

And in that somewhere in the middle, we often find eggs, which, when paired with beans, rice, and salsa, can make an incredibly healthful, satisfying meal in true Latin style. I've included my personal-favorite recipe here for Scrambled Eggs with Black Beans and Sweet Plantains, but I encourage you to mix and match scrambled and fried eggs with red, black, and white beans; vary the kind of rice; and get creative with your choice of salsa. The combinations for fabulous breakfasts are endless.

GINGER-YOGURT BREAKFAST PARFAIT

SERVES 4

½ CUP HONEY

2 TABLESPOONS MINCED
FRESH GINGER

2 TABLESPOONS ORANGE
ZEST (ABOUT 2 ORANGES)

2 TABLESPOONS ORANGE
JUICE

1 QUART GREEK-STYLE
NONFAT YOGURT

1 BANANA, PEELED AND
SLICED

1 MANGO, PEELED AND
DICED

1 CUP BLUEBERRIES

CHOPPED WALNUTS OR
SLICED ALMONDS, FOR
GARNISH

Eating this pretty parfait for breakfast is like starting the day with dessert. It's delicious but really healthy and fresh and packed with protein and fruit.

In a small pitcher or a measuring cup, stir together the honey, ginger, orange zest, and juice until well blended.

In each of 4 parfait or red wine glasses, layer in some yogurt, banana, mango, and blueberries, a generous spoonful of the honey sauce, a second layer of yogurt, and a final layer of fruit and sauce. Garnish with nuts and serve immediately.

PINEAPPLE-GINGER SMOOTHIE

SERVES 1

¹⁄₂ **CUP PLAIN YOGURT**

¹⁄₂ **CUP FRESH OR CANNED PINEAPPLE CHUNKS**

1 TABLESPOON MINCED FRESH GINGER

¹⁄₂ **CUP ICE CUBES**

PINEAPPLE-BANANA GINGER SMOOTHIE

Add ¹⁄₂ banana before blending.

This invigorating breakfast or anytime smoothie is best, of course, with fresh pineapple, but if you don't have any, you can use canned pineapple that has been packed in natural juice. Drain before using.

Purée the yogurt, pineapple, ginger, and ice in a blender until smooth. Serve immediately.

SCRAMBLED EGGS
WITH BLACK BEANS AND SWEET PLANTAINS

SERVES 6

2 TABLESPOONS BUTTER OR OLIVE OIL

8 LARGE EGGS, LIGHTLY BEATEN

KOSHER SALT

FRESHLY GROUND BLACK PEPPER

2 CUPS QUICK BLACK BEANS (PAGE 120)

SWEET PLANTAINS (PAGE 131)

1 CUP BASIC SALSA (PAGE 141)

Here's what to do with leftover black beans. Prepare the sweet plantains and then it takes just a few minutes to scramble the eggs. Serve this with your favorite salsa—I love to use the sweet plantains to scoop it up. This is the kind of breakfast my sons often request for dinner.

In a large skillet, heat the butter over medium-low heat. Add the eggs, season with salt and pepper, and cook, stirring with a wooden spoon, until scrambled, 2 to 4 minutes.

Divide the eggs among 6 plates, spoon black beans and plantains onto each plate, and garnish with a spoonful of salsa.

BREAKFAST
QUESADILLAS

SERVES 4

1 TABLESPOON BUTTER OR OLIVE OIL

4 LARGE EGGS, LIGHTLY BEATEN

KOSHER SALT

FRESHLY GROUND BLACK PEPPER

FOUR 8-INCH FLOUR TORTILLAS

1 CUP SHREDDED MONTEREY JACK CHEESE

2 LARGE VINE-RIPENED TOMATOES, DICED

3 GREEN ONIONS, WHITE AND GREEN PARTS, THINLY SLICED

1 CUP BASIC SALSA (PAGE 141)

My philosophy is that breakfast should be easy.

With just a few basics like eggs, tortillas, and cheese, you can make these quesadillas either as a weekday breakfast-on-the-go or as a festive Sunday brunch. Wrap these in aluminum foil, and you can stick them in your kids' hands as they run out the door to catch the school bus.

In a medium skillet, heat the butter over medium-low heat. Add the eggs, season with salt and pepper, and cook, stirring with a wooden spoon, until scrambled, 2 to 4 minutes.

Place the tortillas on a clean work surface. Sprinkle each tortilla with cheese. Spoon some diced tomatoes on the bottom half of each one, followed by a sprinkling of green onions and a spoonful of salsa. Divide the scrambled eggs among the tortillas and then fold the top of the tortillas over the ingredients to make half-moons.

Heat a dry large skillet over medium-high heat until hot. Heat each tortilla until the interior is melted and heated through, 2 to 3 minutes per side.

Cut each quesadilla in half and serve with any remaining salsa.

MINI ZUCCHINI FRITTATAS
WITH JALAPEÑO

SERVES 6

1 TABLESPOON OLIVE OIL

1 MEDIUM ZUCCHINI, DICED

1/2 MEDIUM YELLOW ONION, DICED

1 RED JALAPEÑO, FINELY DICED

8 LARGE EGGS

1/2 TEASPOON KOSHER SALT

1/2 TEASPOON FRESHLY GROUND BLACK PEPPER

NONSTICK COOKING SPRAY

Baked in muffin tins, these are a cute and simple variation on the traditional Spanish frittata. These are a great make-ahead recipe for brunch for a crowd: Double the recipe and serve these hot or cold.

Preheat the oven to 350°F.

Heat the olive oil in a medium sauté pan over medium heat. Add the zucchini, onion, and jalapeño and cook until the onion is tender and translucent and the zucchini has begun to soften, about 3 minutes. Set aside to cool.

Whisk the eggs with the salt and pepper. Lightly coat 6 standard-size muffin tin cups with cooking spray. Fill each cup halfway with the eggs, then divide the vegetables among the cups and top with the remaining eggs. The muffin tins will be nearly completely full.

Bake for 12 to 14 minutes, until the frittatas are puffed up, firm, and golden brown. Remove from the oven and let stand for a minute to set the eggs. The frittatas will rise quite high in the oven and then fall a bit as they rest. Gently tap the frittatas out of the tin. Serve hot or chilled. The frittatas can be stored, covered, in the refrigerator for up to 2 days.

POWER
BREAKFAST

SERVES 4

8 OUNCES BROCCOLI FLORETS, EACH HALVED LENGTHWISE

1 MEDIUM ZUCCHINI, CUT INTO ¼-INCH-THICK SLICES

1 TABLESPOON OLIVE OIL

12 LARGE EGG WHITES

KOSHER SALT

FRESHLY GROUND BLACK PEPPER

3 CUPS BROWN RICE
(PAGE 126)

1 CUP BASIC SALSA
(PAGE 141)

This is an uber-healthy breakfast of egg whites, vegetables, and brown rice and one of the most requested brunch dishes on my menus. This dish truly demonstrates the power of a salsa. The salsa is what makes eating this breakfast not only doable but really enjoyable and completely satisfying as well.

Set up a steamer and bring an inch or two of water to a boil in it. Put the broccoli and zucchini in the steamer, cover, and cook until tender when pierced with a knife, 3 to 4 minutes.

While the vegetables are cooking, heat a large sauté pan over medium heat. Add the olive oil and egg whites and season with salt and pepper. Cook, stirring with a wooden spoon, until the eggs are white and scrambled.

Put the brown rice into 4 shallow bowls and top with the egg whites, vegetables, and salsa.

PIÑA-COLADA
PANCAKES

SERVES 4 TO 6

2 CUPS ALL-PURPOSE FLOUR

1/4 CUP PLUS
2 TABLESPOONS SUGAR

1/2 TEASPOON SALT

3 TEASPOONS BAKING
POWDER

1 CUP CANNED COCONUT
MILK

1 CUP MILK

3 TABLESPOONS UNSALTED
BUTTER, MELTED AND
COOLED SLIGHTLY

2 LARGE EGGS

3/4 CUP FRESH OR CANNED
PINEAPPLE CHUNKS,
THINLY SLICED

1/2 CUP SHREDDED
SWEETENED DRIED
COCONUT

Studded with sliced pineapple and shredded coconut, these pancakes are delicious for weekend breakfasts. If you don't have any coconut milk, use all regular milk and your pancakes will still be stellar.

In a large bowl, whisk together the flour, sugar, salt, and baking powder. Combine the coconut milk, milk, butter, and eggs in a medium bowl and whisk to combine. Add the wet ingredients to the dry and whisk until just incorporated.

Heat an oiled griddle or large skillet over medium-high heat.

Working in batches, use a ladle to spoon 1/4 cup of batter for each pancake onto the hot griddle. As the pancakes cook, drop some pineapple and a sprinkling of shredded coconut onto each pancake. When air bubbles form on top and the undersides are golden, 2 to 4 minutes, depending upon the heat under your griddle, flip the pancakes and cook for 2 minutes on the other side.

Serve hot.

COCONUT
FRENCH TOAST
WITH MANGO

SERVES 4 TO 6

1 CUP CANNED COCONUT MILK

2 TABLESPOONS SUGAR

4 LARGE EGGS

1 ½ CUPS SHREDDED SWEETENED DRIED COCONUT

6 THICK SLICES CRUSTY BREAD

6 TABLESPOONS UNSALTED BUTTER

RASPBERRY PURÉE (PAGE 180) **OR MAPLE SYRUP**

1 MANGO, PEELED AND SLICED

½ PINT RASPBERRIES

In my house, we make this colorful dish whenever we have people over for brunch. The French toast gets a little sweetness from coconut and a little tartness from Raspberry Purée and diced mango.

In a shallow bowl, whisk together the coconut milk, sugar, and eggs. Spread out the coconut on a plate. Dip the pieces of bread in the egg mixture and then dip in the coconut, amply coating the bread. Melt the butter on a griddle or in a large skillet over medium-high heat. Place the slices of bread on the griddle and cook until the coconut is a golden brown, about 4 minutes. Flip and cook until the other side is golden and the middle isn't soft or soggy, about 4 minutes.

Serve hot, topped with Raspberry Purée, mango slices, and raspberries.

DRAGON
POTATOES

SERVES 6

**2 POUNDS LARGE RED
POTATOES, UNPEELED**

5 TABLESPOONS OLIVE OIL

**3 JALAPEÑOS, SLICED INTO
CIRCLES**

2 CUPS QUICK BLACK BEANS
(PAGE 121)

**1 CUP GRATED MONTEREY
JACK CHEESE**

**4 GREEN ONIONS, WHITE
AND GREEN PARTS, THINLY
SLICED ON THE DIAGONAL**

**1 LARGE VINE-RIPENED
TOMATO, DICED**

This is a much-in-demand breakfast side dish
at my restaurants. It got its name when my sons were young and
thought they could become fire-breathing dragons if they ate
these spicy potatoes. The potatoes are twice cooked: once boiled
and then smashed flat and sautéed. Serve with eggs and a little
salsa alongside, if desired.

Place the potatoes in a large pot of salted water and bring to
a boil over high heat. Cook until they are tender when pierced
with a fork but still hold their shape, about 40 minutes.
Drain, and set aside to cool slightly. When they are cool
enough to handle, smash them with your hands so they are
slightly flattened and chunky.

Heat 1 tablespoon of the olive oil in a small skillet over
medium-high heat. Add the jalapeños and sauté until slightly
blackened, about 3 minutes. Remove from the heat.

Heat the remaining 4 tablespoons olive oil in a large sauté
pan over medium-low heat until hot but not smoking. Add
the flattened potatoes and cook until golden brown, about
6 minutes. Turn and continue cooking until the other side
browns, about 6 minutes more.

Transfer the potatoes to 6 serving plates. Top each with a
scoop of black beans, a sprinkle of cheese, some green
onions, and tomato. Garnish each with the sautéed jalapeño.

SOURCES

ANDRES' LATIN AMERICAN MARKET

1249 Morena Boulevard
San Diego, CA 92110
619-275-6523

Latin American and Spanish foods, including guava paste and yucca

COST PLUS WORLD MARKET

www.costplus.com

Ethnic foods, dishware, and housewares

THE CUBAN FOOD MARKET

3100 SW Eighth Street
Miami, FL 33135
877-999-9945

www.cubanfoodmarket.com

As the name suggests— everything Cuban

DEAN & DELUCA

560 Broadway
New York, NY 10012
800-221-7714
www.deandeluca.com

Specialty foods and kitchenware

ETHNIC GROCER

695 Lunt Avenue
Elk Grove, IL 60007
847-640-9570

www.ethnicgrocer.com

Pantry items from all over the world with a great Latin selection

THE KITCHEN MARKET

218 Eighth Avenue
New York, NY 10011
888-HOT-4433

www.kitchenmarket.com

Mexican and other Latin specialty foods, including chiles, hot sauces, and herbs

MELISSA'S

P.O. Box 21127
Los Angeles, CA 90021
800-588-0151
www.melissas.com
Exotic fruits and vegetables

PENZEY'S SPICE HOUSE

1512 N. Wells Street
Chicago, IL 60610
312-274-0378

www.thespicehouse.com

Amazing chile powders and other spices

SALSA EXPRESS

P.O. Box 1157
Fredericksburg, TX 78624
800-437-2572

www.salsaexpress.com

Salsas, chiles, and other fiery foods

THE SPANISH TABLE

505-986-0243
www.thespanishtable.com
Great Spanish ingredients, including saffron and guava paste

SUR LA TABLE

www.surlatable.com
800-243-0852

Kitchenware and specialty foods

LA TIENDITA MEXICAN MARKET

3851 Clairemont Mesa Boulevard
San Diego, CA 92117
858-270-2221

Mexican specialty food store and meat market

WHOLE FOODS MARKET

www.wholefoodsmarket.com

Organic, gourmet, and ethnic foods

WILLIAMS-SONOMA

www.williams-sonoma.com

877-812-6235

Kitchenware and specialty foods

ACKNOWLEDGMENTS

I have been blessed with not one but two Latina matriarchs, Mom and Tita, whose love and constant support have remained steadfast through thick and thin. Words can't express my feelings for both of you. Thank you to Dad and Paco in heaven. You are both truly missed. Thank you to the rest of my familia: Lee, Julie, Coby, Ava, Erik, Deena, Jackson, Scott, and Marilyn. I know putting up with me through the years has not been easy. And to my new family: Alex, Lauren, Abbie, Kellie, Tara, Big Bill, Michelle, Leah, Mom, Steve C., Steve T., and Gina. If it weren't for my familia and family, my love for food and cooking wouldn't be what it is.

Special thanks to the glue that holds my restaurants and kitchens together: Amalia Romero, Lucy Abarca, Omar Delgado, Edgar Delgado, Neil and Dee Clooney, Kristi Brimm, Carlos, Paulino, Carmelo, Tim, Monia, Jenn, Sara, Tara, and Lucia. I feel so fortunate to have the opportunity to work with all of you. You have been superstars when dealing with the day-to-day restaurant chaos. Thank you to our warrior staff. Thank you to all our loyal customers at the Coffee Cup, Seaside Cantina, Isabel's Cantina, Dragonfly, and Isabel, as well as Chris P. and Danielle at Sin of Cortez.

Thank you to Krakatoa and Olga and Stella Divine Finds for lending earth-friendly furnishings and soulful accessories.

Much love to the girlfriends who love to eat: Elaine, Kathy, Stacy, Cheryl, Shawn, Carla, Monica, Naomi, Christy, Maria, Zoe, and Robii. You are always there for me. Thank you, Marciel, for taking such good care of my boys.

Thank you to the A Team that made this book possible: my agents Lilly Ghahremani and Stefanie Von Borstel at Full Circle Literary, for believing in me; Barbara Newton-Holmes and Kathryn Reed, for coming through and working tirelessly with me to get every word just right; Marcella Marinho, for being so dedicated to me throughout this project; Chef Larry Lewis and the San Diego Culinary Institute, for being so diligent in testing my recipes; Gregory Bertolini, for his gifted eye—you are a talented photographer; everyone at Clarkson Potter; and special thanks to Rica Allannic—a better editor and inspiration could not be found.

Last but not least, thank you to my two sons, Robert and Ryan, who have put up with the crazy, crazy restaurant life I have given you. You are both wise beyond your years. And to my husband, Bill: We have been through enough to fill many lifetimes together. You are my biggest critic and fan all in one. I will love you forever.

THROUGH FIRE AND ICE,

ISABEL

INDEX

PAGE NUMBERS IN *ITALICS* REFER TO ILLUSTRATIONS.